# Theme Games

## LESLEY PINCHBECK

SCRIPTURE UNION

Scripture Union, 207–209 Queensway,
Bletchley, Milton Keynes, MK2 2EB,
England.

© Lesley Pinchbeck 1993

First published 1993
Reprinted 1994, 1995, 1997, 1999

ISBN 0 86201 841 2

British Library Cataloguing-in-Publication Data.
A catalogue record for this book is available from the British Library.

Cover by Mark Carpenter Design Consultants.
Book design and illustration by Neil Pinchbeck.

Phototypeset by Input, London.
Printed and bound in Great Britain
by Cox and Wyman Ltd, Reading, Berkshire.

# CONTENTS

# THEME INDEX

# TITLE INDEX

# BIBLE INDEX

14

# INTRODUCTION

**Why 'theme games'?**

Playing games with children can be much more than just a 'fun time' in a programme of youth work. This book aims to show how the ideas which we try to communicate through Bible study and other teaching materials can be brought alive through games.

Most of the available teaching material for use with children in the 9–13+ age group relies heavily on a high degree of literacy in order to present ideas. We confront them, all too often, with a wall of words: 'Turn to page x', 'Read the story on page y', 'Look up these verses and answer the questions,' and so on. Using games as a teaching aid is a simple, effective and fun way of lowering this literacy barrier, and of capturing the attention and interest of all children. Talking about 'conversion', for example, or reading about the conversion of St Paul can prove difficult concepts for less able or less literate children to grasp. Play a game of 'Conversion volleyball' with these children, however, and ask them what they did in the game and they will say: 'Changed sides.' They are then much closer to an understanding of what conversion means.

If you also play 'Conversion hockey' and discuss the feelings aroused in the course of the game, you will then enable them to relate much more readily to the Bible story of the conversion of St Paul and its consequences and impact on those around at the time.

Games become learning experiences when children discover things for themselves in a real and tangible way. Playing 'Creation Kim's game' makes them look at things around them in a new light, as they begin to experience the reality of what they have been hearing or reading of creation in Genesis. 'God made everything' ceases to be theory and becomes visible fact.

All these games are intended to be supplementary to whatever teaching material is being used; find a game to liven up a rather solid session, or use the ideas here to make more of an already good programme. Add a new dimension to your fun and games.

**What is a 'theme game'?**

Many of the games in this book are simple variations of well-loved old favourites and old-fashioned party games. The latter are often surprisingly popular; in this age of computers, video and disco, party games often seem quite novel to many children.

Whatever the game, or its origin, the importance is in the application – what you do with it – and the discussion and thinking time afterwards. If a child can discover for himself, through thinking about a game he has just played, what the theme of the day's session is to be, that information and the ideas arising are likely to remain fixed in his mind. This is much more effective than any announcement you may make on the matter – a case perhaps of actions speaking louder than words!

## Using *Theme Games*

Each game is laid out in a simple format, with a key guide as to suitability for age groups, group sizes, playing space etc. If special equipment is needed, this is listed at the beginning.

The thematic index is based on the most common subjects in Christian Bible teaching eg sin, salvation, hearing, obeying etc. If you cannot find a theme listed which exactly fits your needs, there is a section at the end of the book on multi-purpose games, which lend themselves to adaptation to fit almost any theme or subject matter.

The games title index should enable you to relocate a game quickly, by title, if necessary.

At the end of each game description, 'Theme points' identifies the major theme and spells out exactly how to use the game to draw out from the group whatever point or theme you are trying to get across. Many games can be used to make several different points: eg there is overlap between hearing, listening and obeying. All these points are listed.

To help you in choosing and using your theme games use this simple check-list of thinking points.

### Think About

**1 What** your theme is to be. This may be very obvious to you, but sometimes it can be difficult to decide exactly what is to be the main point of your study. As I have mentioned, there can be an overlap of several themes in one study. Try to see what it is that God is saying to you, today in that particular session – and stick with it. Too many theme points can be confusing.

### Think About

**2 When** in this session you want to play a game/games. It is often useful to begin your meeting with a 'theme game'. Games make good curtain raisers for any event; they break down barriers of uncertainty and diffidence, and act as a unifying factor drawing the group together in a relaxed manner. When the starting point is also a theme game, you begin with the group already having established in their minds the direction you will now be taking with your Bible study. The session then begins with everyone that much more tuned in and receptive to the points which will then be raised.

A 'games break' during your session can provide a welcome relief for the more energetic and fidgety group members – and their leaders! If the game is also a theme game it means that continuity is kept – the topic is kept alive, and reinforced, by the game they play. You are then able to return to your study session with the group refreshed, and better able to concentrate, having released pent-up energy – and having gained a new slant on your theme.

**Think About**
3 What **kind** of game you need to play? Indoors? Outdoors? Noisy? Quiet? Do I want to liven things up or calm them down? A lively game is sometimes usefully paired with a quieter game. The lively game provides the ice-breaking, warming-up time, and the quieter game brings the players 'down' sufficiently to continue with the session in a constructive manner.

**Think About**
4 How **many** games you want to play? In addition to the point just mentioned, pairing lively games with a 'quietener', or playing more than one game with the same theme and then asking the children to identify the common denominator can be a useful way of drawing the 'theme' idea from the group, rather than just telling them what it is.

**Think About**
5 **Where** you will be playing the game. Some games are obviously best played outside on a fine day (eg water games) but most can be played in whatever space is available. Make sure you have a suitable playing space ready and waiting so that you can go straight into your game. If necessary be ready to organise everyone to stack chairs and clear a space, or to adjourn temporarily to a suitable playing area.

**Think About**
6 The **ages** of your players. Most of the games in this book work well with all children in the 9–13 age group. Many of them also work well with slightly older children. Teenagers vary enormously in degrees of sophistication and attitudes towards games playing. You will know your own group and be best placed to make the final decision, but games marked with the 'OK for teenagers' logo can be used successfully with most older children as well as the younger age group. The age coding on each game will give a guide to any exceptions to the '9–13' norm.

**Think About**
7 The **feelings** of the players. Some children may be reluctant to join in – never force anyone! The whole point of playing a theme game is that everyone should relax, enjoy the fun and see things for themselves. Reluctant games players often get drawn into things, in spite of themselves, when they see others having a good time. Even those hardy characters who remain resolutely aloof will get the point you are making simply by seeing and hearing all that is going on.

**Think About**
8 The **players** themselves. This may seem obvious but it can be easy, when planning a group session, to overlook aspects of some games which could cause problems for handicapped members. This does not necessarily mean that you completely exclude these games from your repertoire; but it does mean that you need to be aware of potential

difficulties and be prepared to think of ways round them. For example, a child with a hearing problem might find a listening game almost impossible. You could include the child in the game quite easily and without embarrassment – another important factor – by giving him a role to play (eg tape-recorder operator, score-keeper, quiz-master etc). The same thinking applies to physically handicapped children who may find very active games difficult. Try pairing them with a 'runner' or 'helper'; appoint them as 'referees' and 'linesmen'. The important thing is to work out in advance what part you will ask them to play, at all costs avoid the last-minute 'Oh dear! What about you?' situation, which helps no one.

## Think About
**9 Numbers** of players. How many will there be? Very small numbers can play most of the games. Even two teams of three work reasonably well. Don't forget to co-opt leaders to make up numbers and balance teams where necessary. Some games may be difficult with very large numbers and you may need to sub-divide the group to play the game effectively.

## Think About
**10 Teams**. Some games have to be played in teams for the game to work: in others teams provide a way of breaking a large group into manageable numbers. Be careful how this sub-division into teams comes about! Best friends tend to hive off together, which is not always helpful, there will inevitably be a lame duck who is left out, the most able and agile members may all end up in one team . . . and so on! It is difficult to achieve fair balance between teams every time, but there are ways of managing fair(er) play.

For two teams the simplest device is probably just to number everyone off – '1, 2, 3, 4 . . .' – and then announce that the teams are to be odds and evens. If you are really cunning (or that desperate?) you can allocate your numbers so that you achieve a balance of abilities etc without the players realising it is happening.

Alternatively, and this is useful for splitting rivals or best friends constructively, pick two children and tell them to pick their team members in turn. Everyone gets picked eventually. If you use this method make sure eveyone ultimately has a turn to be a team picker.

In a really large group where you need three or more teams, you will need some kind of team identification (eg coloured team bands).

## Think About
**11** Your **leaders**. You may be running the session single-handed – make sure the game you choose poses no problems if this is the case. If you have several leaders, make sure that all of those who are helping know what the game is about, what the rules are, and what is the theme point of the day. It may help you to jot down the game title and main points of the game on to a postcard beforehand for quick

on-the-spot reference when your mind goes blank at a vital moment! This is particularly useful if you intend to play more than one game with the same theme.

## Think About

**12 Reactions** to the games. 'Theme points' for each game will give some guidance as to how to use each one sensitively and to make your point. Be alert, however, for group members who may have found your particular 'point' hard to handle. This is especially important in role-playing where emotions may run high. Give everyone the time and opportunity to talk out their feelings and return, emotionally, to the here and now. It is helpful to emphasise the fun aspect of this kind of game: for example 'Conversion hockey' just gets sillier and sillier as it becomes impossible for the losing team to win at all since their star players have 'converted' to the opposition. Emphasis on this will help counteract frustration and aggression felt by some to whom winning is all-important.

## Think About

**13 Competitiveness.** There will always be some players for whom winning will be more important than the game itself. Be alert for these children and try to emphasise the fun aspect to them; don't let over-competitiveness from a few spoil the fun of the majority. On a practical level:

a. If you reward winners (even verbally) then reward everyone else as well for taking part.

b. **Never** belittle a loser – or losing team.

c. Include a variety of games so that different skills are brought to the fore. There is seldom one individual who is the fastest, most agile, has the best general knowledge or memory etc. Use variety to help the group to appreciate each other's differing talents.

d. Whatever skills may be needed, always look for opportunities for the most able to help the less able.

## Think About

**14** What happens **afterwards**. At the end of your meeting it may be helpful to re-cap briefly on any game(s) played earlier. Children who didn't quite see the point at the time may now be able to do so more readily. They may like the opportunity to play the game again if they particularly enjoyed it. Use your discretion here; it can be frustrating to be rushed through a game you are enjoying simply in order to get on with other things. Knowing there will be further opportunites to play for fun at the end could be a great help – and something to look forward to afterwards. You may prefer, of course, to reinforce your theme by playing another, different game as a finale.

## Think About

**15 Equipment.** None of the games call for any specialist or hard-toobtain equipment. If any equipment is required, this is always listed at the beginning of the game description. It is worth mentioning here that foam sponge tennis balls and footballs are much safer and easier to use in a group than the real thing. Inflatable beach balls and balloons can often be substituted for these to make it possible to play almost any ball game indoors. A ball made from (clean!) old socks turned in on themselves and stuffed with socks or tights – a stitch or two secures this nicely – also makes a cheap and cheerful substitute as a ball for an indoor game.

**Think About**

**16 Compiling** your own collection of theme games. You may well have come across a game similar in application to those described here. If you played it, and it worked – save it!

Invent your own! Begin by praying for inspiration, then try to identify the key thoughts and actions involved in your study. Now think about how these could be applied or drawn out of a game. You may then be able to see how an existing game could be used. For example if your theme is 'jealousy', play 'Pass the parcel' and discuss how the losers felt. Add it to your collection!

Finally, it's worth mentioning that although all the players are referred to throughout as 'he' and 'him', this is not intended to imply that girls won't be participating! Please regard this simply as a device to streamline otherwise cumbersome instructions regarding himself/herself/themselves!

# KEY TO LOGOS

OK for teenagers ————————————————— **T**

Suitable for big groups ————————————————— **G**

Needs a big space ————————————————— **S**

Only suitable to play outdoors ————————————— **O**

# 1 BACK-TO-BACK

This game provides a good way of mixing a big group together – try to avoid pairing best friends if you can.

**Equipment required**
None

**To play**
Split the group into two equal teams – use a leader to make up numbers if necessary. Without explaining why, line the teams up facing each other. Then tell everyone to turn round and face the opposite direction and back up so that each team member is now almost back-to-back with a member of the opposite team. There should be enough space between pairs for you to go down the line and question each pair in turn. They must not turn round or turn their heads – if they do, they're out! Eyes front at all times!

Now go down the line and in turn ask each member of a pair a question about their opposite number. Each correctly answered question gains a point for the team. The questions can be repeated, the only important thing is that nobody knows what they will be asked!

*Sample questions*
What colour eyes has your partner?
What colour hair has your partner?
Is your partner wearing something blue? Brown? Green?
Is your partner wearing any jewellery?
Is your partner wearing trainers?
Is your partner wearing a T-shirt?
Has your partner got curly hair?

Improvise if you wish – eg if a child has a slogan on a T-shirt, ask what it is. If he's wearing a badge, ask for a description. Be careful not to ask anything too personal, eg about fatness, skininess, spots or anything like that.

If you have a small number of players you could go back up the line a second time for another round of questions.

**Theme points – Appearances**
How much do we really notice – or care about – people around us? Does the degree to which we're aware of their appearance relate to how much or how little notice we take of what they're like *inside* – their hopes, fears, worries and needs?

Jesus knows and cares about every aspect of every one of us.

● **Appearances, Caring, Jesus knows and cares**

# 2 PASS THE BAG!

This is a very simple, very silly game, best played fairly fast.

**Equipment required**
Cassette player/radio or other source of controllable music, black bin liner containing as many and as varied an assortment of garments as you can manage. (The bag must not be too heavy to pass round!)

*Suggested garments*
All sorts of hats – sun-hats, baseball caps, shower hats, bobble hats – nylon nighties, aprons, scarves, petticoats, waistcoats, gloves, football socks, dress shirts, overalls.
   Anything light-weight and easy to pull on will do nicely.

**To play**
Have the whole group sitting in a circle. Tie the top of the bag loosely. When the music starts the bag must be passed from hand to hand as in 'Pass the parcel'. When the music stops, whoever is holding the bag must untie the top, put a hand in (no picking and choosing – even looking – allowed!) and remove a garment which he must then put on – and keep on – for the rest of the game.
   Play continues until the bag is empty and everyone looks suitably silly. Try to fix it so that eveyone has at least one garment by the end of the game. If you like, you can now call for a fashion parade. Get everyone to walk round the room (together) with musical accompaniment before sitting down and taking everything off again. Be sensitive about this and don't press on if anyone's suffering agonies of embarrassment – but if the mood is right it can be good fun and provide a further laugh all round.

**Theme points – Appearances**
Point out that everyone felt pretty silly by the end of the game. Why? Because appearances matter to us – and to some of us more than others. We want to 'look good' and we often think other people judge by appearances. What does Jesus say about this? God judges us by what's inside, not what's outside. Jesus accepts us as we really are – he doesn't judge us by our looks, or our clothes. You could go on into a discussion about how we judge people by appearances (or not) and how our attitude should be that of Jesus – unconditional acceptance of each other. See Matthew 23:25–28.

- **Appearances, Acceptance, God knows us**

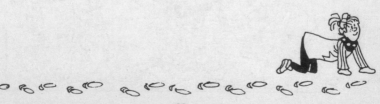

# 3 SIR LAUGHALOT

**Equipment required**
Newspapers, tape, staplers, string.

**To play**
Divide your group into teams of three to five players. Give each team a pile of newspapers and tape, staplers and string.

Tell the group that Sir Laughalot, that well-known knight of old, has been called to a jousting match with the dreaded Sir Morbid – but, horrors, he hasn't a thing to wear! The teams have five or ten minutes to dress their knight in armour suitable for a tournament! The teams pick a volunteer from their number to be Sir Laughalot and concoct a suit of armour out of the newspaper. They can make shields, helmets – whatever they think will be useful.

At the end of the allotted time, call your knights together and elect a champion by popular acclaim.

**Theme points – Armour of God**
Discuss what items of 'armour' the champion was wearing. Most will have a breastplate. Some will have a shield. What pieces are missing? What areas are unprotected? Check with Ephesians 6:13–17 – what is the 'armour of God'? Newspaper armour does not give protection against anything. What does God's armour protect against? Also – picking up the theme of readiness – Sir Laughalot wasn't ready for the big fight. Are we? What are we fighting?

- **Armour of God, Protection, Readiness**

# 4 SPLOSH!

Outdoor Only!

**Equipment required**
One balloon, half-filled with water, per pair of players. *Note*: It is advisable to remove shoes before playing this game.

**To play**
Children pair up and stand in two long lines, an arm's length apart, facing their partners. All the players on one side are given a balloon half filled with water.

On the word 'SPLOSH!' from the leader all the players with the balloons throw them to their partners who must catch them and hold them.

Now all the balloon holders take one step backwards. On the word 'SPLOSH!' the balloons must be thrown again. Burst 'balloonists' are out.

Repeat the procedure until only one pair have an unbroken balloon – they are the winners.

**Theme points – Baptism**
Baptism means 'to immerse in' – some of the players will have come close to it in this game!

You could play several water games (see games 21, 46, 88, 120 and 121) and ask the group to tell you the common theme. Then ask them to tell you other uses for water. Include baptism, and take your study from there. Thirst and drinking can also be used as starting points for Bible discussion – see John 7:27 and John 4:13.

- **Baptism, Thirst, Living water**

# 5 GRAND SLAM

**Equipment required**
Two sets of sixty-six pieces of paper with the books of the Bible written on them: one set in blue and one set in red. Jumble them up in a box or on a table-top at the far side of the room.

**To play**
Two teams, one red and one blue, run a relay race to piece a Bible together. The first team member must find a slip with the first book of the Bible – Genesis – written on it in the team colour. Then the next team member goes to find the next book and so on. The winning team is the first one with the complete, *correct!* sequence in front of it.

The team leader may need a Bible to look up which book teams need to find next.

**Theme points – Bible**
This is simple teaching aid to learn what are books of the Bible and what sequence they are in. It also shows that the Bible is a *collection* of books.

• **Bible, Books of the Bible**

# 6 RECIPES FOR DISASTER

**Equipment required**

Ten different (edible!) substances for a tasting session. Possible substances include:

| | |
|---|---|
| Ground nutmeg | Flour |
| Ground almonds | Desiccated coconut |
| Cornflour | Curry powder |
| Salt | Ginger |
| Sugar | White pepper |
| Brown sugar | Cayenne pepper |
| Lemonade powder | Dried herbs |
| Ground mixed spice | Garlic powder |
| Cocoa | Coffee |
| Dried milk | |

Only a very small quantity of each is required as tasting consists of wetting a finger, dipping it in the powder and then tasting. Have the substances in separate plastic bags or jars with numbers on them, no labels – keep track of what they are!

**To play**

There are several ways of playing this game.

Individuals taste each substance and compile their own lists of 'what they are' and 'what would I use it for' or 'what recipe would I use it in' (eg ginger – cake making/gingerbread).

For a group game, divide into two teams. The team leader keeps the master list of answers and the team members take it in turns to do the tasting. (This works best with large numbers.) If a team member can't guess the substance, the other members can then help out with their ideas.

When everyone's list is complete call the groups together and ask for their findings. These could be written up where they can be seen – then give the correct answers as necessary.

**Theme points – Bible**

Go back to one of the substances on the list – eg curry powder. How much curry powder do you need in a curry? Exactly? What size curry? Why can't you say? Answer – Because we have no instructions. And why were the substances hard to identify? Because we had no labels.

Trying to cook with unknown ingredients and without a recipe book is a recipe for disaster: so is trying to live without instructions for life. The Bible gives us God's recipe for living. See Deuteronomy 5:1–22 and Matthew 5:1–12.

● **Bible, Commandments, Beatitudes, Directions**

# 7 BLINDFOLD BREAKFAST

## Equipment required
For each team you need a bar of chocolate on a plate, knife and fork, die and throwing cup, scarf for blindfold and a pair of gloves.

## To play
For each team put a plate with a bar of chocolate and knife and fork on a chair or table on the opposite side of the room to the players. Give each team a die, throwing cup, blindfold and pair of gloves. It is a good idea to have a referee available to check that the blindfolds are securely tied as required.

The teams commence play, passing their dice round and trying to throw a six. When a player throws a six, he has to put the gloves on and allow the other team members to blindfold him. He is now turned round three times, then the team must direct him to the chocolate without touching him at all. Once he has found the table, the team then tell him where to put his hands to find the knife and fork, and where to aim with the knife and fork to cut the chocolate, spear a piece on the fork, and eat it.

The winning team is the first one to feed their blind man a square of chocolate. Share the remaining chocolate between the team members.

## Theme points – Blindness/sight
Ask the blindfolded players how it felt. Did they keep wanting to peer round the edges of the blindfold? It is frustrating not being able to use your eyes – as well as difficult. Jesus talked about blindness – he also healed the blind. What sorts of blindness does the Bible mention? What is 'spiritual blindness'? Your blind man was able to have breakfast because the team rallied round to help. We are told to help our less able brothers and sisters. We can easily imagine being blind simply by being blindfolded temporarily. It's not so easy to sympathise with people with other problems, such as depression, stress or hidden worries, but we should try to be aware of them and help them too. This game also illustrates trusting – the blindfolded player had to trust the others to lead him safely. We can trust Jesus to lead us safely and keep us safe.

- Blindness/sight, Caring, Helping, Trusting

# 8 CAT AND MOUSE

**Equipment required**
Two chairs, placed about three metres apart in the centre of room; blindfold.

**To play**
One player is chosen to begin the game as the 'cat' and is blindfolded and led to the space between the chairs. The rest of the players are the 'mice' and have to pass between the chairs to the far side of the room without the cat hearing them and catching them. They can go through either one at a time, or three or four can try at once.

**Theme points – Blindness/sight**
Themes here can be blindness – what's it like for the cat to have to rely on hearing alone? What does Jesus mean by spiritual blindness? Some people cannot see and believe in Jesus. They are relying on their own, limited understanding of things – Jesus can help them to see. See John 9 for Jesus' healing of blindness of both kinds.

Another theme picks up on what the mice were doing – trying to avoid being caught. The cat was blindfolded – but God isn't! He sees and knows everything we do and say and think! This is why we need to belong to Jesus. Only as Christians who are forgiven and accepted just as we are, will God accept us as his children.

- **Blindness/sight, God knows all/sees all, Acceptance**

# 9 FUNNY FEELINGS

**Equipment required**
One pillow-case, with identical contents, per team; pencil and paper.

*Suggested contents*

| | |
|---|---|
| Toothbrush | Battery |
| Comb | Empty Coke can |
| Pencil | Carrot |
| Tennis ball | Teaspoon |
| Ping-pong ball | Packet of jelly |
| Nail brush | Cork |
| Marble | Pill bottle |
| Pine cone | Cassette case |
| Clothes peg | Hair slide |
| Acorn | Whistle |

**To play**
Divide the group into teams. Tie the necks of the pillowcases with string so that no one can see the contents. Say that you will give the teams sixty seconds to feel the pillow-case and guess what's in it, they will then have to get together and write a list of the contents. Everyone can feel the contents at once. After sixty seconds take away the pillow-cases and provide pencil and paper. Each team works to produce the most complete list of contents. If you like, you can tell them how many items were in the pillow-case. The winning team is the one with the most complete list. Tip a pillow-case out and hold up the contents one at a time as a visual check-list.

**Theme points – Blindness/sight**
How easy was it to identify things by touch alone? What must it be like to be blind? What does it mean to be spiritually blind? What things are we unable to see if we are spiritually blind? We are like the players in the game, fumbling around trying to work things out by ourselves without seeing clearly what it is we are doing. Jesus can help us see! Look at Luke 4:18; 7:21.

This game can also illustrate what it's like to be limited or disabled in any way. There's a link with God's creation – he enabled us to appreciate creation by being able to see as well as touch, hear, etc.

The theme of 'discernment' – telling things apart – is relevant. We had to rely on sense of touch to tell things apart. What kind of discernment does the Bible speak about (between right and wrong, good and evil)? Jesus can help us here, too.

- **Blindness/sight, Handicaps, Disabilities, Creation, Discernment**

# 10 CATERPILLAR RACE

**Equipment required**
None

**To play**
Divide the group into two teams. *Note*: Girls need to be wearing trousers!

The team members sit in a line, one in front of the other. They put their feet over the shoulders of the person in front and raise themselves off the ground on their hands. When both 'caterpillars' are assembled they 'race' across the room!

**Theme points – Body of Christ**
1 Corinthians 12:12 speaks of the body of Christ as like a single body with many parts. In this race each team formed a single 'body' made up of many parts – none was unimportant, and individual ability was less important than the ability to work together.

The winning team only won because of the efforts of everyone. We cannot say, 'I don't need you,' to anyone who is part of the team – or of the body of Christ. See 1 Corinthians 12:26.

• **Body of Christ, One body/many parts, Working together**

# 11 ESCALATING THREE-LEGGED RELAY RACE 🅣

**Equipment required**
Supply of scarves or ties to tie legs together at the ankles.

**To play**
Form two teams of equal numbers. The race begins as a three-legged race with two pairs from the two teams tied together and racing to far side of room and back.

When they get back another player is added and has his leg tied to one of the other players – it is now a four-legged race!

Play continues in this fashion until the whole team has run the race and sits down together at the starting point.

**Theme points – Body of Christ**
1 Corinthians 12:12 speaks of the body of Christ as like a single body which has many parts. At the end of the race each team formed a single 'body' made up of many parts – none was unimportant, and individual ability was less important than the ability to work together with the other team members.

The winning team only won because of the efforts of everyone. We cannot say, 'I don't need you,' to anyone who is part of the team – or of the Body of Christ. See 1 Corinthians 12:26.

• **Body of Christ, One body/many parts, Working together**

# 12 MINEFIELD

**Equipment required**
None

**To play**
Divide your playing area into three sections, one in front of the other. One section (not necessarily large) is 'home base': the next, wider strip is the 'minefield': on the far side is another, narrower strip which is 'safe haven'. Make the minefield as big as you can with a large group playing.

To begin with, everyone is in home base except for one player, who is 'It' and can only roam the minefield. At the signal to start, everyone must rush from home base across the minefield, while 'It' tags as many players as possible. Once tagged they have to join 'It' and try to tag the other players – but only players in the minefield may be tagged. Once the first rush is over, give the signal again – and everyone must re-cross the minefield to home base without being tagged. The last player – or two – to remain untagged become the first 'It' for another round of the game if you wish to play again.

**Theme points – Captivity/sin**
What sort of things in our lives might be represented by a minefield? What sort of troubles might we encounter? Others tagged you and trapped you in the minefield and we can be led astray and caught up in wrongdoing by others. We should avoid this and set our eyes on the 'safe haven' – life with Jesus.

We should also be careful not to cause others to go wrong. See Romans 14:13.

- **Captivity/sin, Led astray**

# 13 PRISONERS IN CHAINS

**Equipment required**
None

**To play**
Designate one corner or recognisable area as the 'prison'. Outdoors this could be a tree – prisoners have to touch the tree with one hand all the time. Indoors you could do the same with a chair or table. Tell the players that if they are caught (tagged) they will be 'chained up' in prison – touching the tree or chair.

Divide the group into three teams. One team are the 'hunters', the other two are the 'escapers'.

On the signal to start, the hunters all try to tag the escapers. A tagged escaper must go to prison and remain in chains there until a free escaper manages to tag him and thus release the prisoner – who can join the game again.

**Either** play for two or three minutes then stop and count the prisoners. The teams swap sides; the hunters joining the escapers and one of the other teams becoming hunters for the next round. The team which had most prisoners after three rounds is the winner.

**Or** play until all the escapers are chained up in prison and then swap roles for a second and third round of the game.

**Theme points – Captivity/sin**
The game is about 'being caught', 'imprisoned', 'chained up' and 'released'. Jesus talks about 'setting the captives free'. What sort of captives does he mean? What sort of things can chain us up (sin, bad habits, wrongdoing, etc)? Who can release us (Jesus)? How do we avoid being caught (remain in Jesus' hands)? See Luke 4:18, 19.

See also Acts 12:6–7 – Peter in chains. Play this game and ask the group to tell you why Peter was in chains. Where? At whose order? How was he freed?

- Captivity/sin, Peter

33

# 14 GET OUT OF THIS!

**Equipment required**
None

**To play**
Either play with the entire group – it doesn't really matter how large the group is – or split the group into two teams for a team race version.

Either way, the players should stand shoulder to shoulder in a circle facing inwards – or two circles for the team version. Everyone must shut their eyes and put both hands forward into the centre of the circle and grasp two other hands at random. They then open their eyes, and try to untangle themselves without releasing their grasp. For the team version, the two teams race to see which team can get untangled first.

**Theme points – Caring**
The players got into a tangle – some were in more of a twist than others. Some were able to get sorted out relatively easily. Did the freed players advise the ones who were still struggling? Do we try to help those we see with problems? Helping people get untangled sometimes involves 'bending over backwards to help' – literally. Do we put ourselves out to help others, or do we only help when it's no inconvenience to ourselves? What should we do – and what does the Bible have to say? Pick up on how our lives get in a tangle. What sort of things tangle us up? How do we untangle things when we're in a mess? Prayer is vital, as well as help from others.

- **Caring, In trouble, Working together, Helping, Prayer**

# 15 TRIANGLE TAG

**Equipment required**
None

**To play**
Divide your group into teams of four. Three players form a triangle by holding hands, the fourth is outside the triangle.

One player in each triangle is chosen as the 'target'. The outside player has to try to tag the target, the others try to protect him by revolving the triangle and moving about. They **must** keep holding hands. If the target gets tagged then he becomes the outside player and a new target is chosen.

**Theme points – Caring**
The aim of the triangles was to protect their target players. We are told to take especial care of vulnerable members of the church family. See 1 Corinthians 12:22–23. Who might these be (the old, infirm, very young, people with problems)? How might they be tagged (by loneliness, depression, illness, not knowing Jesus in their lives)? How can we protect them (by working together with everyone doing their bit – praying, visiting, caring, sharing, encouraging etc)?

- **Caring, Sharing, Church family, Protecting, Working together, Encouraging, Responsibility**

# 16 CHAMPIONS

**Equipment required**
  Hula-hoops – two
  Pack of cards
  Dried peas and two straws
  Two cups, bowl
  Two books
  Two pens, paper
  Rope for tug of war
  Two round balloons (deflated)

**To play**
Divide the group into two teams. Explain to the group that you are going to find out who are the champions. You will be setting tasks for the teams to achieve, and the teams themselves must choose their own champion to do that task. The two team champions will then compete. No team member may compete as team champion more than once! So they must pick carefully . . .

*The challenges are to*
1. Hula-hoop the longest without stopping.
2. Tell the funniest joke.
3. Build the highest card house in sixty seconds.
4. Draw the best dog or cat.
5. Fetch ten dried peas from a bowl on a table across the room, using a straw. No touching the peas!
6. Arm wrestle an opponent and win.
7. Whistle a recognisable tune – the most easily recognisable and tuneful wins.
8. Walk round the room with a book balanced on the head – no hands allowed. The first to drop their book loses. Increase the pace progressively.
9. Blow up a balloon until it bursts.

The leader reads these out one at a time and as they are called out the teams send a champion forward to compete on their behalf. If there are more team members than challenges, invent a few more. Make sure they include non-physical challenges such as numbers 2, 4 and 7 above.

Finally, end with a mass team-tug-of-war with all members of both teams competing. Assign leaders judiciously to make it as even a match as possible!

### Theme points – Chosen people
How did teams choose their champions? They tried to fit the person to the task. Not everyone is the best at everything – we all have different strengths and weaknesses. The tug-of-war at the end shows what it should be like: we should all pull together – literally – in order for the whole team to benefit.

How does God choose people to work for him? The most obvious people are not always the people most suited to the task. God's chosen 'champions' have included: Jonah, David, Samuel, Moses, Joseph, Daniel, the twelve apostles, Paul etc!

See 1 Peter 2:9. God has chosen us all to be his 'champions' – God's own people, chosen to proclaim the wonderful acts of God.

• **Champions, Chosen people, Working together**

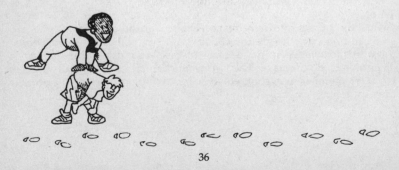

# 17 THE CHOSEN FEW

**Equipment required**
List of 'elimination factors' – or make these up as you go along (avoiding anything too personal or sensitive).

*Sample elimination factors*
Anyone wearing black shoes
Anyone with green eyes
Anyone wearing something red
Anyone with two brothers

**To play**
This can be played as a prelude to other games if you have plenty of time and want a novel method of choosing one player as 'It' in a tag game. It can be played with any number of players.

If the 'elimination' factors are being used *ad lib*, it is fairer if the person calling them stands with his back to the group, otherwise . . .

The leader stands at the front, facing the whole group, who should also stand. The leader announces that he is looking for a mystery person – 'X'. Nobody knows who he is or what he looks like, yet, but there are a few clues. Produce the list and begin to read; as you read, anyone who possesses the characteristic mentioned must sit down. Eventually you will be left with two or three players, and finally one. If the final two or three are disqualified unexpectedly together, then try again with another factor to find 'X'. This is a silly game that needs to be played for laughs, rather than as a serious competition.

**Theme points – chosen by God**
Matthew 22:14 reads, 'Many are invited, but few are chosen.' This relates to the parable of the Wedding Feast, but you could use the link of many being called but gradually being eliminated. What were the eliminating factors with the game/with the wedding guests?

Luke 13:30 reads, 'Those who are now last will be first, and those who are now first will be last.' How did it feel to be made to sit down early on? Unfair? Jesus promises justice in the Kingdom of Heaven – those who truly belong to him will not be pushed aside here!

'Elimination factor' links with Achan's sin following the fall of Jericho and how he was picked out – Joshua 7. See also the link with Gideon and the Midianites (Judges 7) and how he chose his army.

- **Chosen by God, Wedding feast, Achan, Gideon**

# 18 KNOCK IT OFF!

**Equipment required**
Four tablespoons, two tennis balls.

**To play**
Divide the group into two teams (A and B). Two players face each other, each with two tablespoons – one in each hand. Each player has a tennis ball on one spoon. On the word 'Go' they 'fence' with their empty tablespoons and try to dislodge their opponent's tennis ball while trying to keep theirs on the spoon. The first player to lose his tennis ball is the loser.

Team A choose their first fencer and send him out. Team B must now pick a suitable opponent to fence with him. When they have fought the first round the winning team scores a point. Team B then chooses a second player and team A selects their opposition – and so on.

Play continues with teams alternating at being first to choose a player. The game finishes when everyone has had one turn.

**Theme points – Chosen by God**
How did teams choose their players? They tried to match the players to the opposition – the appropriate person or 'champion' for the moment. God chooses people who are 'right' for the particular moment. Go on to discuss how God chooses people; talk about people he has chosen and how we are all 'chosen' if we are followers of Jesus. We are all chosen for a purpose – what is God's plan for us?

- **Chosen by God, Champions, Chosen people, Working together, God's plan**

# 19 MUSICAL KNEES

**Equipment required**
Chair for each player less one, music.

**To play**
Set the chairs out in a line, facing alternate directions, or set them in a circle, seats facing outwards.

The whole group stands in a circle around the chairs. When the music starts they move round the chairs; when it stops everyone tries to sit down. Everyone must sit down – if there is no chair they must sit on someone's knee! Continue to play, removing one chair each time until the whole group has to sit on one chair on each other's knees!

**Theme points – Church family**
This is a completely silly game that is good to play in conjunction with another game with a similar theme in order to draw out the theme point, which is that they all need each other in the end – no one was unimportant. They had to work together and help each other. This is what we are supposed to do as members of the body of Christ – the church family.

Also, on the theme of trusting, they had to trust each other not to 'let them down' – literally. We should be able to do this. We can trust Jesus not to let us down.

• **Unity, Working together, One body/many parts, Trusting, Church family, Co-operation**

# 20 THAT'S US!

**Equipment required**
Narrative – see below. The basis for this game is a narrative which centres on what happened when a (mythical!) church family went on an outing. The narrative given is a rough guide. Adapt and alter it to fit your own situation, eg the vicar could be a minister, priest, or leader; churchwardens could be elders; Mothers Union could be Ladies Circle or Mum's Club; choir could be musicians etc.

This version contains the names of eight people and groups:

a. Vicar
b. Churchwardens
c. Sparklers
d. All-Stars
e. Lazer Group
f. Mothers Union
g. Choir
h. Scouts and Guides

## To play

Before you begin, allocate the identities to individuals or small groups of children. Explain that when they hear 'their' names mentioned they must jump up, shout, 'That's us!' turn round and sit down again. If the word 'church' is mentioned, *everyone* must jump up, shout, 'That's us!' turn round and sit down again.

Before you begin, have a quick roll-call to ensure everyone knows what to do. Then tell the story of: 'The CHURCH Outing'. (Words in capital letters are buzzwords – emphasise if necessary! Italicised words should be read very quickly.)

Let me tell you the story of what happened when the whole CHURCH had an outing last year.

Well, first of all we had to decide where to go. The VICAR said we should put it to the vote, the CHURCHWARDENS agreed and the whole CHURCH was consulted.

The SPARKLERS wanted the seaside, so did ALL-STARS and the LAZER group. The CHOIR wanted a theme park and the SCOUTS AND GUIDES agreed. The MOTHERS UNION didn't like theme parks and voted for the seaside like SPARKLERS, ALL-STARS and the LAZER GROUP. The CHURCHWARDENS agreed – then the VICAR had a good idea. We went to the seaside for our CHURCH outing – which pleased SPARKLERS, ALL-STARS and the LAZER GROUP no end. The MOTHERS UNION went shopping, the CHURCH-WARDENS went fishing and the CHOIR got together with the SCOUTS AND GUIDES and went to the *fun-fair up the road, so the whole CHURCH had a good time; the VICAR, the CHURCHWARDENS, SPARKLERS, ALL-STARS, LAZER GROUP, MOTHERS' UNION, the CHOIR and SCOUTS AND GUIDES and everyone.*

### Theme points – Church family

This is just played for fun, as a silly, rather noisy game. The point is that the church is everyone, together, and when they all jump up and shout, 'That's us!' when the word 'church' is mentioned, they are acting out the truth. You could ask, 'What is the Church?' The body of Christ is one answer – but in practical terms its 'everyone who belongs to Jesus in this place – that's us!'

● **Church family, Body of Christ**

# 21 SLIPSOAPS

**Equipment required**
Each team needs one new bar of household soap (other soaps can be used but household soap comes in big bars that are harder to handle when wet) and one bucket half-filled with water.

**To play**
The aim of the game is to traverse the course before the other team. Mark out a start and finish.

Give each team a bar of soap and a bucket of water. They all line up at the start. One player in each team is elected to go first. He wets his hands and the soap and 'shoots' the soap as far as he can (no throwing allowed) in the direction of the finishing line. Another player must catch the soap before it hits the ground! If it hits the ground, the soap-shooter must try again. If a team-mate catches it, he stays where he is, soaps his hands and repeats the process with the other team members attempting the catch. Make your course long enough for all the team members to have a go at shooting the soap.

The winning team is the one which is the first to shoot the soap across the finishing line – to be caught by a team member behind the line.

**Theme points – Cleanliness**
Ask who has clean hands! Everyone! You can now draw parallels with what the Bible has to say about being clean, eg how Jesus makes us clean from sin. (See John 15:3.) Being 'clean inside' is just as important as being clean outside – but what does this mean? (See Mathew 23:25–26.) Baptism is an outward sign of this cleansing. See Luke 3:3, about John the Baptist, and Acts 22:16 – Paul's account of his own baptism/cleansing from sin.

- **Cleanliness/baptism, Sin, John the Baptist, Paul**

# 22 HIT THE DECK

**Equipment required**
Two sets of slips of paper with the ten commandments on them, one set in red, one set in blue.

**To play**
Two teams, one red and one blue, run a relay to fetch the coloured slips they need, one at a time, from a jumbled heap face up on the far side of the room. The first team to collate all ten commandments in the correct order, wins.

The team leader may use a Bible to look up the correct sequence if you wish. See Deuteronomy 5:1–22.

**Theme points – Commandments**
This game is a simple teaching aid as to what the commandments are, and in what order they were given.

• **Commandments**

# 23 SIT!

**Equipment required**
Two sets of slips of paper with the ten commandments on them, one set in red and one in blue. Mix them up in a hat. Have two chairs (one per team) at far side of the room.

This game really needs ten players in each team. It doesn't matter if there are only enough players for one team of ten: play in exactly the same way, but with one set of paper slips and one chair.

**To play**
On the word '**Go**' all the players run to the hat and take a slip. They must now sort themselves out, first into colours and then into the order of the ten commandments. (If there's only one team they won't need to sort themselves into colours first!)

The person with the first commandment (No. 1) must sit on the chair; No. 2 sits on the knee of No. 1 and so on up to ten. The first team correctly seated, wins.

Number the commandments on the slips if you want a quick game. Leave the number off if you want a more thoughtful game, but put a Bible on each chair so that the teams can look it up.

**Theme points – Commandments**
This game is a simple teaching aid as to what the ten commandments are, and the order in which they were given.

• **Commandments**

# 24 CONVERSION HOCKEY

**Equipment required**
Newspaper for each player, balloon, four chairs to make two 'goals'.

**To play**
Place two chairs at either end of the playing space to mark the 'goals'. Divide the group into two teams. Equip each player with a rolled up newspaper 'hockey stick'. Tell them they have two minutes to play each way. The team with the highest score wins.

Take note of who is/are the best player(s) in the winning team and when you blow the whistle for half-time tell them to change sides and join the losing team. Ignore cries of, 'Unfair!'

The losing team should now win as they have extra players – and all the best ones!

**Theme points – Conversion**
Ask the teams how they felt about what had happened. How did the team that was winning at first feel about losing their star player(s)? How did the losing team feel about gaining them? This can be related to conversion, especially that of St Paul (see Acts 9).

See point five – 'Reactions' – in the Introduction. Make sure everyone gets the point, but also make sure no one is left harbouring any grudge about unfairness etc. St Paul's friends must have felt a bit cheated!

Conversion is about changing sides, and not everyone will understand what's happened.

● **Conversion**

With a little ingenuity this can be played almost anywhere, even in amazingly small spaces.

**Equipment required**
For really small playing areas use a balloon for your ball (and have a few spares in case of it bursting). Otherwise, for an indoor game a beach-ball – the inflatable sort or sponge football – works best.

You will also need a length of string or rope to make your 'net'. Tie this across the room/hall/playing space just above head-height.

**To play**
Begin by dividing into two roughly equal groups and playing a three minute game of volley-ball. The aim is to keep the ball airborne; it must clear the net and it must not touch the ground. Points are scored by getting it over the net and on to the ground on the opposing side. If it goes under the net when hit, it scores against you. A three minute limit will provoke some really frantic play!

At the end of that time, announce that there will now be a slight change of rules. For the next round, once the ball has been hit, the player who has hit the ball must duck under the net – and join the opposing team!

**Theme points – Conversion**
Ask the group what differentiated the two games? You should get the words 'changing sides'. Ask for another word meaning 'to change sides': Someone will mention conversion. Each time the ball was hit, someone converted to the other side. How did the teams find this? Confusing? Think now about other conversions, especially Saul/Paul, and how this must have seemed to those around at the time. See Acts 9.

• **Conversion**

# 26 CIRCLE SITTING

**Equipment required**
None

**To play**
Everyone stands in a tight circle all facing the back of the next person. Everyone must now sit down – on the knees of the person behind them. It can be done!

When this is achieved you can try some instructions – stand! – turn! – sit!

**Theme points – Co-operation, working together**
Achieving the 'sit' depends entirely on co-operating with each other. Nobody is unimportant and individual ability is less important than helping the person next to you in the circle.

You could play this in conjunction with the 'Escalating three-legged relay race' and the 'Caterpillar race' and ask the children to tell you what the games have in common. Co-operation and consideration for others should come up.

- Co-operation, working together, One body many parts

# 27 LINK-UP TAG

**Equipment required**
None

**To play**
Players form pairs, back to back, with arms linked at elbows. One pair of players are 'It'.

Play tag exactly as usual; tagged players are out. The last remaining untagged pair become 'It' for the next round. Elbows *must* remain linked throughout.

**Theme points – Co-operation, working together**
Both the players who were 'It' and those trying to escape being tagged had to co-operate closely with their partners in order to play the game. We must work together with one another – beginning with those closest to us – if we are to obey God and live in peace with other people.

- Co-operation, Working together

# 28 COUNT THE COST

**Equipment required**
Bag of shopping. Make the items as varied as possible and keep a list of the contents and their price.

*Suggested items*

| | |
|---|---|
| Packet of crisps | Camera |
| Bottle of squash | Packet of seeds |
| Can of beans | Tin of dog food |
| Watch* | Bar of soap |
| Tube of toothpaste | Can of air freshener |
| Paperback book** | Roll of sticky tape |
| Biro | Battery |
| Packet of chewing gum | |

\* use catalogue to check price of this sort of item
\*\* cover or erase price on back

There should be at least as many items as there are group members, and a minimum of about fifteen items.

Pen and paper for each player, star stickers or a red marker pen for the leader.

**To play**
The leader produces the bag of shopping and announces that the group is going to be tested for 'cost consciousness'.

The bag is placed on a table, and three group members step forwards. The leader produces the first item of shopping and places it on a table where everyone can see it; the three players have ten seconds to individually write down their estimates of the cost of the item. If they haven't a clue they should guess. Now ask for their answers, reveal the price, and stick a star/draw a red star on the papers of the two closest estimates. The third player resumes his seat and is replaced by another. Any 100% correct estimate gets two stars! Play on until all the shopping is stacked around the table, and then offer a bonus of five stars to any group member who can estimate most closely the total cost of the whole lot.

Tot up stars to find the winner.

**Theme points – Cost of discipleship**
Who wins? Whoever does the most shopping, most likely. This is an introduction or game-break on the theme of 'counting the cost' of discipleship. Who is most likely to know the true cost of discipleship/following Jesus? Whoever tries to follow him the most closely. You very soon come up against decisions involving self sacrifice etc – this is the cost. Go on from here. See Philippians 3:7 and Luke 14:25–33.

• **Cost of discipleship, Counting the cost**

# 29 CREATION CONVEYOR BELT

**Equipment required**
Two deep bags or sacks, one being full of manufactured and natural objects.

**To play**
Play this exactly as for 'Conveyor belt' (game 122) but using a mixture of manufactured and natural objects (eg leaves, shells, twigs etc). Use up to about twenty objects for this game.

**Theme points – Creation**
As with 'Creation Kim's game' (game 30), first ask the children to list all the things which passed before their eyes and which God made. *Then* point out that ultimately everything comes from God and is his creation. Ask them to list the rest of the objects.

• Creation

# 30 CREATION KIM'S GAME

**Equipment required**
Tray or table with about twenty objects on it – include some natural objects such as leaves, conkers, shells, stones, flowers, etc. Cover this with a cloth.

**To play**
Either give each player a pencil and paper or have a black-board or OHP available to write things up yourself.

Everyone is to gather round the tray or table. The cloth is removed for thirty seconds and then replaced. The children must now either write down individually, or tell you to write down, everything on the tray that God has made!

**Theme points – Creation**
The children will all recognise that the stones, shells, leaves etc are part of God's creation. How many realise that *everything* on the tray has ultimately been provided by God also? Now see if they can name everything else.

• Creation

# 31 ELEMENTARY!

**Equipment required**
Tennis ball.

**To play**
All the players except one stand in a circle, facing inwards. One player starts off standing in the centre, holding the tennis ball.

The centre player throws the ball to any player in the circle, simultaneously calling either, 'Earth!' 'Air!', 'Fire!' or 'Water!' The chosen recipient must catch the ball and respond with something connected with whichever word is chosen – simultaneously throwing the ball back. Allow a count of five between catching and returning the ball. A player who can't think of a response in time, or who responds with something irrelevant or that has already been said, becomes 'It' at the centre of the circle.

Examples of responses might be:

Earth – dirt, garden, plants, clay, stones
Air – oxygen, wind, gales, breathing
Fire – flames, burning, heat, barbecue
Water – wet, sea, river, washing, drinking

**Theme points – Creation**
God says, 'The world and everything in it is mine' (Psalm 50:12). Earth, air, fire, water – all are part of God's creation. So too are all the responses that the players made. Link this with the theme of creation. See 1 Corinthians 10:26.

Fire, air and water also are symbols of the Holy Spirit. Ask the group to recall some of their responses, write them down, and go on from there into your Bible study or discussion of the Spirit of God blowing like the wind; being like fire (Pentecost, the burning bush, pillar of fire etc); being like water (river of life, water of life etc). You steer the discussion whichever way is appropriate.

- **Creation, God made everything, Holy Spirit, Wind, Fire, Water**

# 32 CROSS TAG

**Equipment required**
None

**To play**
One player is chosen as 'It', the rest scatter. When 'It' is chasing somebody, if another player manages to run between him and his quarry, then 'It' must now chase the person who crossed in front of him. As soon as there's a wide enough gap again between pursuer and pursued another player can do the same. The idea is that all the players co-operate to 'stay alive'. In practice, the cross-runner will often miscalculate his chances and be tagged himself. Either play an elimination game, or play that anyone tagged plays the next round as 'It'.

**Theme points – Cross**
This game of tag features an element of potential self-sacrifice. Were some players more willing to take risks than others? Rescuing someone in peril of being tagged meant you were more likely to get tagged yourself – unless someone else rescued you.

We have someone who stepped in and rescued us – who died for us. His name is Jesus. The game is called 'Cross tag' because those who wanted to 'save' a player had to cross the path of the chaser. Jesus went to the cross to save us. We should be willing to put the interests of others before our own.

- **Cross, Safety, Saviour, Self-sacrifice, Salvation**

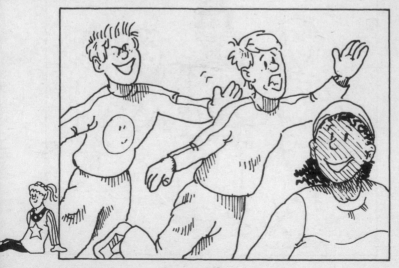

# 33 HARE AND HOUNDS

**Equipment required**
None

**To play**
The whole group scatter and stand still. One player is chosen to start the game as the hare; another starts the game as the hound.

The hound must chase the hare in and around the group of scattered players. The hare is free to tag any stationary player at any time, whereupon the tagged player now becomes the hare and must run leaving the former hare safely in his place. If the hound tags the running hare, then he becomes the new hound and a new hare is chosen – the old hound joining the scattered group. If the hound is in difficulties – if your playing area is large it can be quite hard to catch a hare – then have two hares and two hounds at once.

**Theme points – Cross**
The hares escaped being caught by getting someone else to take their place. Jesus took our place on the cross so that death can't catch us. Sin has no power over us. Also pick upon the theme of help in trouble – the hares found help at hand in other players. In trouble we find help from each other and from Jesus. Prayer is relevant here.

● **Cross, Jesus, Sin, Help, Prayer**

# 34 POLICE!

**Equipment required**

Large assortment of brightly coloured and 'silly' clothing, eg odd socks, two different shoes (one boot, one slipper, silly hat (shower cap?), scarf, gloves (different colours!), shorts (to be worn outside trousers). Have accessories too, eg sunglasses, bright red lipstick (use on nose if you like! for painted on freckles), a wig, umbrella, balloons, teddy.

A volunteer leader dresses up beforehand in all this silly gear, but *none* of the group must get a glimpse – this is important!

**To play**

Have the whole group sitting in a circle and announce to them that before you begin, you have something rather important to tell them. You than go on to say something along these lines:

'There was a robbery last night at my house, someone's pinched all my best clothes! He even took my teddy bear! I shall have to call the **POLICE!**' As you get to the word 'police', shout out it out, and your accomplice should burst in, run round the group shrieking and cackling like a maniac – and zoom out of the door again. (Your accomplice should remain outside for a moment longer.)

Into the stunned silence (?) you now say, 'That was him! Quick – write down a description for the police!' At this point have the group divide into two teams who must then compile as comprehensive a list as possible of the suspect's appearance within a given time limit – three minutes or so. Alternatively you can have a master list pinned up and ask the group to tell you what the suspect was wearing and write it up yourself.

At the end of the time limit, say that you will now call the **POLICE!** At this signal your accomplice should run back into the room and this time stand at the front with you while you check off which group had the fullest, most accurate list – or what it was they didn't remember for your master list.

**Theme points – Day of the Lord**

You can use the shock effect of this game to draw parallels with the idea that 'the Day of the Lord will come as a thief comes at night' (1 Thessalonians 5:2). What effect did it have? It took you by surprise, so much so that it was hard to think straight. This is what Jesus was warning us about – we should be prepared for his unexpected return.

You may like to us this game to link with other observation type games, to point out that God knows everything about us – 'every hair on your head is numbered' – right down to the colour of our socks! And nothing about us is unimportant to him.

- **Day of the Lord, Jesus' return, God knows us**

# 35 DIFFICULTIES

## Version one

### Equipment required
Ping-pong balls (one per team), teaspoons (one per team member).

### To play
The teams line up with all the team members facing forwards, each holding a teaspoon in the teeth by the handle. The team leaders at the front of the line are each given a ping-pong ball.

At the signal to start, the ping-pong ball must be passed down the line from teaspoon to teaspoon, to the last person in the line, who then runs to the front and passes the ball back down the line again.

The ball must remain on the teaspoons at all times – no hands allowed! If it falls off it is retrieved and replaced and game continues until a winning team completes the relay.

## Version two

### Equipment required
Three ping-pong balls per team, one plate per team.

### To play
Teams line up as before and the player at the front of the line is given a plate with three ping-pong balls on it.

At the signal to start, the front players from each team must race, with the plates balanced on their hands like waiters, to the far side of the room, round a chair and back to their team. The plate is then passed to the next player in the line and first player retires to the back of the line.

The game continues until the whole team has run the course. No hands allowed! Dropped balls must be picked up and replaced before continuing.

## Version three

### Equipment required
One balloon and one yogurt pot per team.

### To play
Teams line up as before. The front player of each team is given a balloon (inflated!) and a yogurt pot, or plastic disposable cup.

At the signal to start, the first player in each team must run to the far side of the room, round a chair, and back to his team while balancing the balloon on the pot.

No hands allowed! Balloons are to be retrieved and replaced at point where they are dropped. The game continues until each team member has run the course.

## Theme points – Difficulties

Play two of these games, or all three, or similar games of your own devising. Ask the group if it easy. Some may say 'Yes' – most will say 'No'. Ask the group – how did you overcome the problems you faced? (Probably by being careful, going slowly, concentrating, co-operating.) Tell the group that you are going to look into how we can overcome difficulties in our lives with Jesus' help – being careful, concentrating and co-operating all come into it as well! See 1 John 5:5 and Revelation 21:7 for God's promises to those who do persevere.

- **Difficulties, Co-operation, Working together**

# 36 DIRECTIONS

**Equipment required**
None

**To play**
The four corners of the room are designated North, South, East and West. Make everyone repeat these, pointing to each in turn to fix them in their minds.

A caller in the centre calls any one direction, ie 'North!' 'South!' 'East!' or 'West!' and everyone must run to that corner. The last person to reach it is out, and anyone who goes to the wrong corner is also out. Continue calling randomly and quickly.

If the children get too clever, try calling 'North-east!' or 'South-west!' as a tie-breaker at the end. The last person not out wins, and can become caller for another round, if you like.

**Theme points – Directions**
Often people who are out by going to the wrong corner have done so simply by following someone else – point this out. It's like this in life too – 'going wrong' often comes by following the crowd and not thinking for ourselves. Wrong 'directions' can lead to sin.

Where do we go for directions in our lives? Who can help us orientate ourselves correctly? The Bible and Jesus are our guides.

* **Bible, Jesus the way, Sin, Directions, Commandments, Beatitudes**

# 37 QUICK DRAW

**Equipment required**
Large sheets of paper or wallpaper, felt pens.

**To play**
Divide your group into teams. One member from each team leaves the room temporarily, or closes their eyes, while you hold up a piece of paper with one word on it – the object they must draw. Once the rest of the players know what it is, the artists may return, or open their eyes again. Objects could be:

| | |
|---|---|
| Fried egg | Bicycle |
| Wellington boot | Dustbin |
| Deck chair | Egg beater |
| Light bulb | Telephone |
| Screwdriver | Walkman |

At the signal to start, team members take it in turns to give instructions to their artist, who must endeavour to draw exactly what he is told. Instructions must only relate to the drawing, not the object. For example: draw a straight line; draw a circle at the bottom; draw a line across the top. Anyone issuing a giveaway instruction, such as 'draw a light socket', loses that game for their team. The aim is for the 'artist' to guess what they are drawing!

Have a good long list of objects so that everyone gets a turn at being the 'artist'.

**Theme points – Directions**
Ask the team how success was achieved in this game. Probably it was by **following instructions carefully** but also by **giving the right directions** – the one was no good without the other. We can find the right directions for life in the **Bible (the ten commandments, Jesus' words, Sermon on the Mount** etc) but unless we follow them carefully they won't do us much good. **Hearing and obeying** also relevant themes. See Psalm 119:105, 'Your word is a lamp to guide me, and a light for my path.'

- Directions, Hearing, Obeying, Bible, Following, Commandments

# 38 NOISES OFF

**Equipment required**
Pencils and paper. Either a large empty box or a curtain plus noise-making equipment or a tape of pre-recorded noises plus a cassette player. Making your own tape of sound effects need not be difficult. Noises to record could include:

a. A paper bag bursting
b. Water running from a tap
c. A door closing
d. Keys jangling
e. Footsteps
f. Water boiling in a kettle
g. A book being shut quickly
h. Newspaper rustling
i. Milk bottles clinking together
j. Someone eating crisps

Keep a list of noises as you record them so that you can identify them later! Leave short gaps between your sound effects.

Alternatively you could rig up a curtain or use a large cardboard box as a screen behind which to make some of the noises listed above. You will need more 'transportable' noises produced when you:

Cut paper with scissors
Pour water into a glass
Open a packet of crisps
Strike a match

**To play**
Either give everyone a pencil and paper or divide them into groups and give each group a piece of paper and a pencil. Tell them that you have made a tape of 'noises off' but you have forgotten what they are. You will play it and see if they can identify them for you.

Play the tape, pausing briefly between each sound effect so that they have enough time to write down what they think they've heard. Don't pause too long, keep it moving, and tell them to have a guess at it if they're not sure.

When you have finished, rewind the tape and go through it again, asking the group to tell you what they thought they were hearing for each sound. If you chose to play in groups, they can score points for each correct answer.

**Theme points – Discernment**
Listening is a major part of this game. Listening carefully and not being distracted by those around you – this is how we should listen to God. Discernment also comes into it here, how do we tell noises apart? How do we tell God's voice from other, misleading voices? What is discernment? It is telling things apart.

Blindness is a related theme – it is not so easy to identify things if we cannot see as well as hear, and spiritual blindness can be brought into this. Also we need to *see* God at work as well as hear his voice. God gave us our senses – he gives us the ability to see and hear him as well.

● **Hearing, Listening, Discernment, Blindness/sight**

# 39 PHEW!

## Equipment required
Pencil and paper. Strong-smelling substances in screw-top jars.
Number the jars. Possible substances are:

| | |
|---|---|
| Curry powder | Chopped mint |
| Moth balls | Soap powder |
| Chopped onions | Dried Lavender |
| Grated orange or lemon rind | Garlic |
| Vinegar | |

You don't need a great deal of each one, just enough to give a good
aroma when the lid is removed. Pop each jar into a paper bag so that
the contents are not visible, and secure the bags around the jar necks
with rubber bands.

## To play
Have the group seated in a circle with a pencil and paper each. Tell
them that you're going to see how many things they can recognise
simply by smell! Each player in turn must close their eyes as you
unscrew the jar tops one at a time and pass them fairly swiftly round
the circle under their noses. They must write down, in turn, what it
is they think they've just been smelling!

When you have been through all your collection of odours, go
through them again and ask what the children thought they were. It
gets harder as you go on because your nose get confused!

## Theme points – Discernment
This is just a silly game, but the point can be made that although we
can identify some things by smell alone, life is much easier when we
can also see and hear and touch as well. We need all the senses God
has given us for discernment – telling things apart. What is the spiritual
discernment we read of in the Bible? It is telling good from evil and
right from wrong. See the previous game and play them both to
discover the common theme of discernment.

Blindness is a related theme. When we can't see we are limited in
what we can tell about the world about us. If we are spiritually deaf
or blind we are limited in what we can see and hear of God.

● **Discernment, Blindness/sight, Hearing, Senses**

# 40 DISTRACTION RACE

**Equipment required**
Each team needs either a book or a tablespoon and tennis ball or a teaspoon and ping-pong ball.

**To play**
Form the group into two teams. One player from each team must run to the far side of the room and back with a tennis ball balanced on a tablespoon or a book balanced on their head or a teaspoon held between the teeth with a ping-pong ball balanced on it. A second player takes over as in a relay race.

While the relay is in progress two members of each of the teams must run alongside the opposing team member and pull faces, tell jokes etc in an attempt to distract them and make them drop the ball or book. *Note*: They must **not** touch the player in any way.

If the ball or book is dropped the player must return to the beginning and start again.

The winning team is the first one whose members all successfully complete their turn.

**Theme points – Distractions**
Phillippians 3:14 reads, 'I run straight towards the goal in order to win the prize.' To win, you have to concentrate 100% on the job in hand, keep your eyes on where you are going and ignore the antics of those around you. Sometimes it's better to go slowly and get there safely. Paul tells us to 'keep our eyes on the goal' – to keep looking to Jesus and not be distracted by the world around us.

- **Distractions, Eyes on goal/Jesus**

**Equipment required**
A rolled-up newspaper for each player, a balloon (and a few spares) and string or long scarves to tie players together.

**To play**
Divide the group into two teams and pair each player with an opponent. Either tie them together at the waist, back-to-back, or make them link arms at the elbows, back-to-back. Goal-keepers are also paired in this way.

Put two chairs at each end of the room for goals and play as for 'Conversion hockey' (game 3). Three minutes each way is enough.

**Theme points – Disunity/discord**
Ask how it felt to play this game Annoying? Frustrating?

If you play this in conjunction/with one of the 'link-up' games (numbers 27 and 95) or other 'co-operative' games, you can make the point of how difficult it is to work and live in peace with someone who is not pulling the same way. This comes at the 'working together – unity in the body' theme from the opposite angle to the other games. See Matthew 5:9.

- **Living in peace, Working together, Co-operation, Disunity/discord**

# 42 THREE-LEGGED FOOTBALL

**Equipment required**
Sponge football, two chairs for goalposts, scarves or string to tie the players together.

**To play**
Divide the group into teams and pair them off with members of the opposing team. Tie two opposing players together back to back – or get them to link arms at the elbows back-to-back. These are the goalies. All the other players are tied together at one ankle in pairs.

Play football for three or four minutes. Whichever player was the last to kick the ball into the goal is deemed to have scored a goal.

**Theme points – Disunity/discord**
How did it feel to be playing like this? Frustrating? How easy is it to work or play as a Christian when others are constantly 'pulling the other way'? Life in general and church life in particular are easier when everyone 'pulls' in the same direction. What sort of problems occur in the game? In life discord makes for arguments, bad feelings, bruises. We are told to live in peace and harmony with each other – this is why! It's not always easy, though.

- **Disunity/discord, Peace, Harmony**

# 43 PASS THE PARCEL

**Equipment required**
Music, a parcel wrapped in multiple layers of old gift wrap, newspaper etc with each layer taped or tied with wool. Put a bag or tube of sweets in the centre, to be shared at the end. Wrap this in distinctively coloured paper so that you will be aware of the point when it has been reached. You could include a few boiled sweets in between some of the layers.

**To play**
Play 'Pass the parcel'. When the final layer is revealed, halt the game and don't let the person holding it unwrap the parcel until you have discussed the theme point with the group. Then let the parcel be unwrapped and the sweets shared with all the group members.

**Theme points – Envy/jealousy**
Ask the winner how he feels. Pretty pleased? Ask the other group members how they feel. Put out? Envious? Jealous? Some will say, 'It's not fair.' Here is your introduction to a discussion of these emotions and the problems they bring. You could use Bible stories such as that of Cain and Abel (see Genesis 4:1–16) or the 'Who is the greatest?' argument (see Luke 9:46).

This game also illustrates sharing as a positive antidote to envy and jealousy and as an aid to living in peace with our neighbours.

• **Envy/jealousy, Sharing, Cain and Abel**

# 44 UNEXPLODED BOMB

**Equipment required**
Large ball or cushion; list of questions. These may be general trivia-type questions or general knowledge Bible questions. Music tape.

**To play**
The whole group sits round in a circle. Explain that the ball is a bomb and it must be passed round from hand to hand while the music plays. (No throwing.) If you get caught holding the bomb when the music stops you must answer a question correctly in order to stay alive! If you get the answer wrong, the bomb 'explodes' and knocks you out of the game.

Pitch your questions at the level of individual players – it is helpful if the bomb does not explode too soon.

**Theme points – Eternal life**
Ask how you managed to stay alive in this game. By getting the answers right! What is the question that we need to 'get right' in order to 'stay alive' – ie to have eternal life? It's the question that Jesus asked Peter: 'Who do you say that I am?' (Luke 9:20). The answer is in 1 John 5:12, 'Whoever has the Son has this life.'

You can either play until a pre-set number of players are out or make the questions so easy that you can end the game at your discretion by asking a really difficult one. Answering Jesus' question is both the easiest and hardest thing to do. Why?

- **Jesus God's Son, Eternal life**


# 45 WHAT'S MY LINE?

**Equipment required**
Slips of paper with various occupations written on them. Include a few silly ones if you like, eg feather-duster maker, as well as doctor, policeman, garage mechanic etc. The last slip should be 'evangelist', to make your theme point evangelism.

**To play**
Each child takes it in turn to be given a slip. They then mime briefly their occupations.

The rest of the group can ask up to ten questions in order to work out what it is. The child may only answer 'Yes' or 'No'. If the group can guess correctly that child scores a point. This can be done in two teams.

**Theme points – Evangelism**
By the time the child has mimed the occupation of evangelist *and* answered ten questions this should be fairly well fixed in their minds!

- **Evangelism**

# 46 FIRE!

**T**

## Indoor version

### Equipment required
Two buckets of water, two saucepans or 4 litre ice-cream tubs, two plastic drinking cups.

### To play
Form the group into two teams. Announce that they are fire-fighters racing to put out a fire. Each team sits in line on a row of chairs with a bucket at one end and a saucepan or ice-cream tub at the other. Team leaders (sitting next to the bucket) are given one plastic cup each. All remain seated throughout.

On the word 'Go' team leaders fill the cup, which is then passed along the line to the player at the other end who empties it into a saucepan. The cup is then passed back empty.

The winning team is the one which fills the saucepan first. If you like, the filled saucepan can be passed along the line to the team leader who then stands up, to win.

## Outdoor version

### Equipment required
Two buckets of water, two ice-cream tubs or saucepans, four plastic drinking cups.

### To play
You need two teams, who stand behind a line; two buckets of water placed some distance away; two empty ice-cream tubs just in front of the line.

Players run a relay with a plastic cup in each hand, run to the bucket, fill the cups, run back, tip them in the tub and pass the cups to the next player.

The winning team is the one that fills the tub first or fetches the most water in a given time limit.

### Theme points – Eyes on Jesus/goal
Ask the group what was the key to winning the game. Co-operation and working together should come up. Also, going steadily was more effective than rushing madly. See Hebrews 12:1 and 2, 'Let us run with determination the race that lies before us. Let us keep our eyes fixed on Jesus.'

Ask what other uses are there for water apart from fire-fighting. Washing is one of them – this links with the theme of baptism. The word 'baptise' literally means 'to immerse in' – some of them will have come close to it in this game! You can then go on with a discussion of various aspects of baptism.

- **Eyes on goal/Jesus, Water, Baptism, Sin**

# 47 FILL THE BUCKET

**Equipment required**
Bucket, large number of fairly small balls (tennis balls and ping-pong balls are ideal).

**To play**
The bucket is placed in the centre of the room and must not be touched or picked up at any point. It is full of balls of all sizes.

One player must try to empty the bucket by picking up the balls and throwing or rolling them away one at a time. The rest of the group have to try and re-fill the bucket. Change the 'emptier' frequently to keep the game moving. Give them a time limit of sixty seconds each if you like.

To play this as a team game have one team providing a succession of 'emptiers' and the other team filling the bucket. Switch over when everyone in the first team has had sixty seconds as an 'emptier' and count how many balls are in the bucket. The team with the least balls left in the bucket wins.

**Theme points – Filled with the Spirit**
See Ephesians 5:18. Paul tells us to 'be filled with the Spirit.' (Better translated as 'Go on being filled . . .') Life and our imperfect natures mean that, like the bucket, we need constant replenishing. How do we 'leak'? What sort of things 'drain' us?

God is the one who pours out his Spirit and helps us to remain filled with his presence.

- **Filled with the Spirit, Holy Spirit**

# 48 FISHY BUSINESS

**Equipment required**
Objects to be fished out of the river. Make these as varied as possible and include a few cardboard cut-out fish shapes. Objects could include:

Boots
Shoes
Old stuffed toys
Empty plastic bottles
Plastic cups

Use anything which could be tied to string and fished out of the river. Pile these in the centre of the room. You also need two rulers and lots of string, as long a length as possible, and at least as long as the length of the room. Tie one end of the string firmly to the rulers.

**To play**
Divide the group into two teams and tell them that they are going fishing. Two volunteers – one from each team – go to the far side of the room and sit on two chairs. This is the riverbank. They are given a ruler and string each – they are the fishing rods. The rest of the team members must remain on the other side of the room. To start fishing, each fisherman must cast his line towards his team. One team member from each team must rush forward and tie an object from the river on to the free end of the line. He must then go back to his team and wait while the fisherman reels in his catch. He does this by winding the string round the ruler. *Note*: No overarm hauling is permitted! The line must be wound up properly. When the catch is in the fisherman detaches it from the line and waves it in the air. This is the signal for the player who attached it to race over and take the rod and become the next fisherman. Play continues until all the team members are safely on the bank. (The last object is fixed on the line by the first fisherman.)

**Theme points – Fishers of men**
See Matthew 4:18–22 and Luke 5:1–10.
Who were the fishermen with Jesus? How did they come to know Jesus? What did he say they would be catching? In the game the fishermen 'caught' team members as well as an assortment of fish and other objects. We are told we will be 'fishers of men' if we follow Jesus. What does this mean? The children didn't always land a fish in this game – boots, shoes etc turned up as well. We meet disappointments when we go fishing, but we persevere – the game parallels life here.

• **Peter, James, John, Fishers of men**

# 49 FOLLOW THIS

**Equipment required**
None

**To play**
This game is similar to 'Simon says' but consists of actions only. One person is selected as leader. The leader initiates a series of quick changing actions, eg patting head with the left hand then with the right hand, hands up, hands down, put an arm out etc.

The group must copy this sequence exactly. Anyone who makes a mistake is either out or becomes next leader.

**Theme points – Following**
Success depends entirely on keeping your eyes on the leader and doing exactly as the leader does. This is like following Jesus. We must keep our eyes on him and do as he does and not be distracted by things around us.

You could pick up on the theme of sin, which is disobeying the leader/Jesus.

● **Following Jesus, Eyes on goal/Jesus, Sin**


# 50 CONDUCTOR

**Equipment required**
None

**To play**
Explain that you are forming a band and one of the group is going to be the conductor. One player leaves the room or closes his eyes. A second player is then chosen as the conductor and begins miming an imaginary instrument. The rest of the players, all sitting round in a circle, join in and imitate the instrument!

The first player is called back, or opens his eyes. When the conductor changes instruments everyone else must follow suit immediately – but without giving away who it is they are following. The first player stands in the centre and tries to identify the conductor. If he is successful then the conductor has to leave the room while a new conductor is chosen and the game begins again.

**Theme points – Following Jesus**
The game centred round following the conductor – but without letting on who you were following. Is this how you follow Jesus? It shouldn't be! We should want it to be obvious who we were following and why. How do we give ourselves away as following the conductor? How do we 'give ourselves away' as followers of Jesus?

● **Following Jesus, Witnessing**

# 51 FOLLOWING ON

**Equipment required**
None

**To play**
The whole group sits round in a circle. One player is chosen to start the action. He performs a simple action such as tapping a foot or clapping hands. The next player – sitting on his left – must now perform that action and add to it another, different one. The next player, on his left, now has two players to copy, and two actions. Play continues as fast as possible round the circle. See how far you can get without someone forgetting an action or making a mistake. If someone makes a mistake in the sequence, then they now initiate a new sequence and play starts again.

Alternatively you can play this as an elimination game with a final play-off between two players. This could be a grand finale after playing it the first way a few times for fun.

**Theme points – Following Jesus**
The players had to follow the actions of the others – exactly. We should follow the actions of Jesus as well as his words! What are these? What kind of actions would we perform to follow those of Jesus? If we make a mistake we get another go! Jesus forgives us and wants us to try again. See John 12:26, 'Whoever wants to serve me must follow me' and Matthew 16:24.

- **Following, Actions, Mistakes, Forgiveness**

# 52 FRUIT SALAD

**Equipment required**
None

**To play**
The whole group sits round in a circle and one player begins by saying, 'On the fruit salad tree grow x' and names any fruit (eg apples). The next player has to say the same and add after 'x' another, different fruit (eg apples and bananas). Play continues with each player repeating, 'On the fruit salad tree grow' – followed by the list of previously mentioned fruits, in the right order without leaving any out, and all different. If a player gets the order mixed, leaves one out, repeats a fruit or can't think of another, that round of the game ends. Tot up how many fruits were growing on the tree at the end. Then play another round, with the next player in the circle starting a new 'fruit salad tree'. Play at least three rounds and see what is your record number of fruits on a tree.

**Theme points – Fruitfulness**
Go on from this game to a discussion of what the fruit of the Spirit is. Why 'fruit'? What are the special characteristics of fruit? They take time to grow – and everyone is attracted to them when they're ripe. They're good for sharing, and they keep you healthy! Are there similarities between our lives and good fruit?

Alternatively you could discuss fruit growing. Can you just leave a fruit tree to grow by itself? No – it needs tending, protecting from pests, watering in dry weather – and pruning! This can lead into a discussion of John 15:1–10.

● **Fruitfulness, Father/gardener**

# 53 OH MUMMY!

**Equipment required**
One roll of cheap loo paper per team playing. If you choose to begin with the 'Unwrapped' skit you will also need a piece of fancy giftwrap big enough to wrap all the loo-rolls you will be using, plus ribbons, bows, tinsel, etc to decorate the parcel.

*Unwrapped!*
This skit is optional. You will need an accomplice – either another leader or a group member primed beforehand. Gather the group together, sit them round and announce that you are going to play a great game – but first you have a presentation to make. You then produce a (previously concealed) parcel, which is dazzling to behold, with every trimming imaginable. Hand this to your accomplice with a flourish and make a short speech along the lines of . . .

'We really appreciate your help with this game and we're sure you will find this gift totally brilliant.'

Your accomplice makes a great show of being overwhelmed and exclaims about the beauty of the parcel and the wrappings – and then just sits, with the parcel on his lap, waiting for you to continue. So you say, 'Well – aren't you going to open it then?'

'What, *open* it? *Spoil* it?'

'Yes – open it!'

'Do you want me to open it? (*to the group*)

'Yes!' everyone choruses!

He then opens the parcel slowly and dramatically – to reveal the contents! When the hilarity subsides, he then says, 'Great! Just what we need to play the next game.' Then you proceed to explain and play 'Oh Mummy!'

## To play

Divide the group into teams, each with one roll of loo paper. The teams choose a volunteer to be their mummy. Explain that they will be racing to wrap their mummies completely from head to foot in the paper. Each team member will have twenty seconds wrapping time in turn. Broken ends must be tucked in securely and the paper must cover the whole player – except for eyes and nose. The winning team is the one to use up all their paper first. Then let them start!

When the game is over and one team has won, allow the other team(s) to finish and then announce stage two of the game. The teams must stand back and the mummies must break free when you say 'Go!' The winner will be the one who is completely disentangled first.

## Theme points – Gifts of the Spirit

Ask the group what the skit at the beginning and the game itself had in common – unwrapping. Point out that the parcel itself was no use until it was opened up – then the contents were useful to everyone. The mummy needed to get unwrapped to win, and to rejoin the group.

We all like getting surprise gifts, but the gifts God has for us are even better! What are they? How can we find out what they are? (And what does it mean to 'unwrap them'?) How can we use them for the benefit of everyone? You can also pick up on the theme of the release of captives. The mummy was all tied up: what things can keep us tied up and ineffective as Christians? How can we 'break free', like the mummy?

- **Holy Spirit, Gifts of the Spirit, Release/captives**

# 54 POST THE PARCEL

**Equipment required**
Old newspapers, sticky tape, string.

**To play**
Divide your group into teams of at least five and allocate each team a table with a pile of old newspapers, sticky tape and string. The tables should be at one side of the room. A leader should be seated at the far side of the room with a rolled-up newspaper. He is the post office franking machine!

The groups should each choose a group member to be wrapped into a parcel – the smallest and lightest member for preference.

At the signal to begin, both groups begin to wrap their parcel (leaving eyes and nose free). The parcel should sit hunched and clasp his knees to make this easy. The aim is to produce a parcel that is wrapped securely enough to be carried to the post office and be franked – with the rolled-up newspaper! – and delivered back to base. The winners are the first back to base with a securely wrapped parcel.

It is a good idea to make them put their hands up when they're ready to go to the post office so that you can check that the parcel really is securely and completely wrapped, apart from eyes and nose. A parcel which comes undone halfway must be put down (gently!) and repaired before progressing any further.

When all the parcels have been delivered, give a signal and the first group to unwrap their parcel completely and all sit down gain another point.

**Theme points – Gifts of the Spirit**
We all like getting parcels! But they're not much use to us until they are delivered and unwrapped. You couldn't win the game until the parcel was opened. The gifts of the Spirit are no use unless we seek them, and 'unwrap' them and use them.

What are the gifts? What is in God's parcel for all of us? Unwrap them – find out about them – and ask him to show you how to use them. See 1 Corinthians 12:4–11 and Romans 12:6–8. You can pick up also on the theme of trusting. We trust the post office to deliver our parcels. The 'parcel' has to trust that he won't be dropped! We should be able to trust ourselves to each other. We can trust Jesus.

- **Gifts of the Spirit, Trusting**

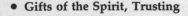

# 55 RUN FOR IT!

This is also known as 'Chinese laundry'.

**Equipment required**

A list of items or characteristics which the group members might reasonably be expected to possess and have on or with them at your meeting. Possible items include:

| | |
|---|---|
| A (clean!) handkerchief | Something green |
| A white sock | Slip-on shoes |
| A shoe-lace | Blue socks |
| Hair elastic | A sweatshirt |
| A pair of glasses | A cardigan |
| A button | A T-shirt |
| A necklace | A nail file |
| Blue eyes | A comb |
| Brown eyes | A pencil |
| Something red | |

**To play**

Divide your group into teams of up to ten members. Appoint a leader for each team. Explain that you are going to call an item on your list and each group must locate a person within the group who possesses that item. The leader takes that member by the hand and together they race to touch the wall on the far side of the room. The first leader and member to reach the wall scores a point for their group. You will need someone to arbitrate and keep score.

**Theme points – Gifts of the Spirit**

There are several different angles on this game. Obviously, the themes of hearing, listening, and obeying all apply, but you could also use the game to illustrate the fact that we, as a church, are one body (one team) and that it is only when we share what we have – the gifts of the Spirit working together – that we function as we should. See 1 Corinthians 12:7 and Romans 12:6–8.

Readiness is another relevant theme. In the game it's no use standing there thinking, 'Oh yes, I've got that,' you must be ready to act when called upon – not just for your benefit but for that of the whole team as well. See Matthew 25:1–13.

- **Readiness, Hearing, Listening, Obeying, Gifts of the Spirit, Working together**

# 56 GIVEAWAY GRAB

This game is played in two stages – A and B. Whichever team wins stage A is unlikely to win stage B as well, which is part of the fun – and helps make your theme point.

**Equipment required**
Tea-trays, dried peas or Smarties, straight drinking straws, two bowls or plastic boxes.

**To play**
Place a couple of tea-trays on a table and empty a fairly large quantity of Smarties or dried peas on to them. Several feet away, put a table or chair with an empty bowl or plastic ice-cream box for each team.
   Divide your group into teams and give each team member a straw. You also need one person (perhaps a leader) to be 'Poor Peter' or 'Poor Penny'.

*Stage A*
At the signal to begin, everyone rushes to the tea-trays and tries to pick up a pea or a Smartie by sucking on the straw. They then rush to their team bowl and drop it in. It must remain on the end of the straw the whole time – no hands allowed. The game continues until the trays are empty and you have a pea-count to see which team has grabbed the most. If you prefer a marginally quieter game, have the team members run in turns to the tray instead of a free-for-all.

*Stage B*
Tell the children that although they have done well, what about 'Poor Penny'? Produce your volunteer, who should have an empty bowl and look suitably miserable. 'Poor Penny' has nothing at all – they've grabbed the lot. So you announce that you are now going to have a race to see which team can be the first to transfer their entire pea collection into Penny's bowl! Then seat Penny where the table and trays were for the first round and play again. The odds are obviously in favour of the team which lost the first round by grabbing the least.

**Theme points – Giving**
There are many ways of emphasising the points of this game. The Bible tells us not to grab more than we need, but to share with those in need. Jesus told the rich young man to share everything he had with the poor (see Matthew 19:16–24). We are told to give generously (see 2 Corinthians 9:7). The widow gave everything she had (see Luke 21:1–4). Draw out whichever aspect you wish to emphasise. Point out that the ultimate winners were not the ones *with* the most but the ones who *gave* the most.

- **Giving, Riches, Sharing, Fair shares**

# 57 WHO?

**Equipment required**
Paper, pencils, a hat or box.

**To play**
Provide each player with two pieces of paper and a pencil. Tell them to write the numbers 1–6 down the left hand side of one piece. Nobody should be able to see anyone else's paper.

While you read out the following questions, the players write down their preferences against the numbers on their pieces of paper.

1. What is your favourite meal?
2. What is your favourite colour?
3. What is your favourite TV programme?
4. What is your favourite animal?
5. What is your favourite singer or group?
6. What is your favourite hobby?

Everyone must write their name at the foot of the page and fold their paper in half and put it in a hat or box.

Shake the box, then take out a piece of paper at random and say, 'Guess whose . . .'

1. Favourite meal is . . .
2. Favourite colour is . . . etc

Everyone must write down who they think it is.

Progress like this until the box is empty, making sure you keep the papers in the order in which you took them out of the box or hat. Now see how many people scored 100%!

If you have a large number of players you can play in two teams. The aim is to correctly identify the preferences of the opposite team members!

**Theme points – God knows us**
Unless your group is very small and the children know each other very well, not many players will get all the answers right. God knows us inside out. He knows all these things about every one of us – and more – as a father knows his child. We are God's children (see Romans 8:15, 16).

- **God knows us, Father/gardener, Jesus knows and cares, Children of God**

# 58 ALL CHANGE

**Equipment required**
None

**To play**
One player is chosen as 'It' and temporarily leaves the room. While he is absent the group decides on a change to make either in the room or within the group. Changes could be: moving a pile of books from one table to another; opening or closing a window; turning an object upside down etc.

If you chose to have changes within the group, have them seated in a circle and, for example swap shoes from one player to another; have two players change seats; put a book on one player's lap; have two players link arms; have one player take a jacket off etc.

'It' returns and tries to identify the change. When he is successful, another player takes his place for another round.

**Theme points – God sees all**
See Psalm 139: 'You know everything I do; where could I go to escape from you?' We are not always very observant of things and people around us. God sees and knows everything! We sometimes think that if no one notices something we do which is wrong (sin) then we are 'getting away with it', when in fact God has seen, and God knows.

- **Observation, God sees all**

# 59 BEANS IN THE JAR

## Equipment required
Several jars. (A pair of scales is an optional extra.) Fill or half-fill the jars with a variety of things, eg Smarties, haricot beans, dried peas, marbles, buttons, wrapped toffees etc. Count them as you fill the jars! Write down how many of each item each jar contains. Number the jars.

## To play
Each player has to write down the jar number and then estimate how many beans etc the jar contains. For an extra twist they must also write down what they think the contents of the jar weigh.

When everyone has finished, first announce the number of contents and then go through the jars one at a time weighing the contents on a pair of kitchen scales. See who has the most correct estimates.

To play this as a team game, divide the group into small teams – threes and fours are enough – and allow them to decide collectively on an answer.

## Theme points – God sees all
God does not need to count or weigh to know all about us. He is all seeing and all knowing. See Luke 12:7, 'Even the hairs of your head have all been counted.' God cares about us.

- **God sees all, God knows us, Jesus knows and cares, God cares**

# 60 HAVE YOU HEARD?

**Equipment required**
None

**To play**
This is a very simple game, best played sitting in a circle. Players take it in turns to pose questions and answer them. Alternatively, have the players in two teams facing each other; teams take it in turns to pose a question and to answer one. For example:

**First Player**: 'Have you heard the bad news?' (*Invents something, such as . . .*) 'There was an earthquake in our town last night!'

**Second Player**: 'Yes – but the good news is' (*Invents a reply such as . . .*) 'there's no school today. It fell down!'

If you play in teams you could give each team a couple of minutes grace before you start in which to compile a list of 'Have you heard' disasters.

Each time a team comes up with the 'good news' it scores a point. If they can't think of any they lose a point!

When you are ready to finish, call for silence and then say:

'Have you heard the bad news? We're all sinners and we're all going to die!'

Then ask if anyone can tell you the Good News. Prime another leader to answer here if no one responds.

'The Good News is that Jesus has died in our place and we are forgiven and are alive in him – forever.'

**Theme points – Good News**
This game is fairly self-explanatory and can lead in to the good news of Jesus. You may also want to point out that this is what the word '**gospel**' means.

• **Good News, Gospel, Eternal life**

# 61 PASS IT ON!

This is sometimes known as 'Chinese whispers'.

**Equipment required**
None – but see below.

**To play**
The whole group sits in a closely-packed circle. The idea is that one person turns to the next on the left and whispers a phrase in his ear. He then has to turn quickly to the next person on his left and 'pass it on' in a whisper. It doesn't matter if he doesn't understand what he thinks he's heard – he just passes on what it sounded like!

You may like to prepare a set of slips of paper with simple tongue twisters on them and allow the children to pick one out of a hat as a starter phrase.

Suitable tongue-twisters might be:

a. She sells sea-shells on the sea shore
b. We shall see the sun shine soon
c. Slim Sam slid sideways
d. Cheap ship trips
e. Six thin thistle sticks
f. The sixth Sheikh's sixth sheep is sick

Alternatively allow them to think of phrases of their own, or use Bible verses.

The last person in the circle has to say out loud what they think they heard.

**Theme points – Good News**
By the time the message reaches the end of the line it will not sound quite the same – especially if the circle is large and the whisper travels fast. Several points can be made here. The question: 'What is the message that Jesus wants us to pass on?' will lead to themes of Good News, gospel, salvation. You can also use the game and its consequences to point to the importance of speaking up clearly for Jesus so that the message is heard plainly and not confused or distorted in any way. Half-truths and half-heard messages can be damaging, eg the idea that 'Easter is when Jesus died' without recognition that Easter is also when Jesus rose from death.

• **Good News, Gospel, Salvation, Hearing, Whole truth**

# 62 BELL TAG

**Equipment required**
Small bell, blindfolds for all but one of the players.

**To play**
Everyone must be blindfolded, except one player, who is handed the bell. The players disperse round the room and the player with the bell must walk, run and sidle about in between them. He must ring his bell at regular intervals. Any blindfolded player who manages to tag the player with the bell, takes the bell and hands his blindfold over in exchange. Play then proceeds as before.

**Theme points – The good shepherd**
The players had to listen hard and attempt to find and follow the player with the bell. In a flock of sheep, the oldest and wisest sheep will sometimes have a bell round it's neck. she will be known as the 'bell-wether' – the other sheep follow the sound of the bell and keep together and keep safe. Jesus is our 'Good Shepherd' (see John 10:1–16) and we should follow the sound of his voice. We should listen for Jesus and try to find him and his way for us in life.

This game links to other themes too. What is it like to be the only person who can see? What is it like to be blind? Seeing in a world of blindness gives you an unfair advantage, and we are told to help others see – to share the privilege of knowing God and seeing his hand at work. Blindness can be frustrating – we try to find the bell-holder but are limited in our ability to do so. We need the help of the Holy Spirit to see and understand God's word to us. Spiritual blindness and Jesus as sight-giver can also be discussed.

- **The good shepherd, Listening, Following, Blindness/sight**

# 63 COLLISION COURSE

**Equipment required**
Chairs, books, sponge balls, small table etc to create an obstacle course in the centre of your playing space. Blindfolds.

Assemble an obstacle course with enough space for a child to walk between the various objects, but arranged at random so that some turning and twisting is necessary.

**To play**
Divide the group into three or four teams and have team members line up on one side of the room. One member of each team steps forward to be blindfolded. Make sure these are secure. At the signal to start, the blindfolded players must make their way across the obstacle course as fast as they can with their arms folded. The other team members must shout directions – and warnings – to their own team member. Anyone who knocks into an obstacle, steps on a book or kicks a ball loses two team points each time. You need an eagle-eyed referee – or two if possible.

As soon as the blindfolded players reach the far side of the room they remove blindfolds, run back to their team and blindfold the next team member. Check again that the blindfolds are secure.

The first team to get all its members across scores ten points, but any penalty points incurred by collisions must be taken off this. Which team wins? Not necessarily the first across – a very slow and careful team with sharp ears may win over a slapdash all-out to win team which crashed into everything *en route*.

**Theme points – Guidance**
With several teams all shouting instructions at once it is necessary for the blindfolded payers to listen very carefully and only respond to *their* instructions. We need to listen hard for Jesus' voice. What other conflicting voices are there in the world today? (Materialism, greed, selfishness, envy etc will be mentioned.) We can collide with any of these things at any time, unless we keep on listening to Jesus' voice. 'Winning the race' depends on this rather than crashing on blindly doing things our way. More haste can mean less speed, in life as well as in this game.

How do we hear Jesus? Sometimes he speaks through those around us – like our team mates in the game who were trying to help us. Sometimes he speaks through God's word – the Bible. If we know what the Bible says, we will be guided by the right voices. See Colossians 3:15.

- Guidance, Sin, Envy, Jealousy, Listening, Bible

# 64 PASS THE BALL

**Equipment required**
Tennis balls – one per team.

**To play**
Divide your group into teams. Give each team a tennis ball and sit the teams on chairs in lines or circles.

At the signal to start, the players with the balls must pass them on, either down the line of players or round the circle – using only their feet to hold and pass the ball. Dropped balls should be retrieved and replaced at the point of dropping. When the ball has reached the end of the line or has gone round the circle it must now be passed back again under the chins of the players, held between chin and neck, no hands allowed. The first team to get the ball back to the start wins.

**Theme points – Handicaps**
Was it easy? No! Life has its difficulties too. The teams overcame their difficulties in order to try to win. We can overcome life's difficulties, and Jesus will help us. Prayer is one way we have of finding this help. Also – picking upon the theme of handicaps/disabilities – not having the use of our hands limits us tremendously.

- **Handicaps, Difficulties, Prayer, Disabilities**


# 65 CRAB-SCUTTLE RELAY

**Equipment required**
None

**To play**
Divide the group into two teams and line them up. The first team member bends down and puts his right hand between his knees and grabs the left hand of the player behind him. The two run like this to the far side of room and round a chair and run back.

The second player, still holding the first player's hand puts *his* right hand between his knees and links up with the third player in the line – all three now run the course.

Continue in this fashion until one whole team has completed the course and sits down again at the Start.

**Theme points – harmony**
We are told in 2 Corinthians 13:11 to 'agree with one another. Live in peace.' We can only do this if we co-operate with each other and – in this game literally! – bend over backwards to help each other in life's race!

- **Harmony, Peace, Co-operation**

# 66 JIGSAWS

**Equipment required**
Whole-page pictures of people, not necessarily famous, cut out of magazines and colour supplements: two pictures per team playing. If there are also pictures on the reverse then either stick blank paper over them or scribble over the reverse so that it is obvious which is the right side. Cut the pictures into about four or five straight-edged pieces. Dice.

**To play**
Divide the group into teams. Each team needs a table or similar flat surface on which to assemble their jigsaws. On the far side of the room place an ice-cream tub on a chair, one for each team. Each tub contains the scrambled pieces of two pictures.

On the word 'Go' the teams commence throwing the dice in turn. Anyone throwing a six runs and grabs a piece of jigsaw and the teams compete to be the first to completely unscramble the mixed-up pictures and re-assemble them correctly.

**Theme points – healing/wholeness**
The teams were making the pictures whole. They were also unscrambling some mixed-up people! How can we be made whole? How can people be 'mixed-up' in real life? Wholeness is healing, and Jesus can make us whole. Sometimes we get mixed-up ideas about God and about life in general. Jesus can unscramble us – if we ask him. See Acts 9:32–35 for an example of Peter bringing wholeness to a paralysed man with the words, 'Jesus Christ makes you well.'

- **Healing, wholeness, Jesus heals, Flawed images**

# 67 JUMPING JACK

This is a version of 'Beetle drive'.

**Equipment required**
Large sheet of paper and thick felt pen plus dice and throwing cup for each team. 'How to score' diagram – see below.

**To play**
Pin the pieces of paper up where they can be seen by everyone. Pin up a large sheet of paper with a matchstick person drawn on it (include hands – five short lines – and feet – two oblongs). Against each part of the body write the following numbers with arrows to indicate which part they represent: body = 6, head = 5, arms = 4, legs = 3, hands = 2, feet = 1.

Divide the group into teams and give each team a die, a throwing cup and a felt pen. They should sit on the floor or round a table. Explain that they are going to see which group can be the first to complete a drawing of 'Jumping Jack'. They must start by throwing a six for the body, and then progress through the other parts. They need to throw a 4, 3, 2 and 1 twice – one for each arm, leg, hand and foot. When the team member throws the right number he grabs the pen and rushes to draw the relevant part on the team paper. Play stops until he rejoins the group. The game ends with the first completed 'Jumping Jack' figure.

**Theme points – Healing/wholeness**
Congratulate the team which completed their figure. Point out that they are the only ones with a whole figure – the other(s) are incomplete and need a few more tries before they can be made whole.

How can we be made whole? What sort of things damage people and leave them in need of wholeness? Jesus makes people whole. The word 'heal' comes from a word meaning 'whole'. It is obvious what the incomplete figure(s) need to be whole – it may be less obvious what we need to be whole. Some healing needs to take place inside rather than outside – in our minds and spirits as well as our bodies. Jesus can do it! God says, 'I am the Lord, the one who heals you' (Exodus 15:26).

- **Healing, Wholeness, Jesus heals**

# 68 JACOB'S LADDER

**Equipment required**

Twenty-four stacking chairs, die and throwing cup, list of numbers – see below. If space is limited, sixteen chairs will do; if chairs are not available use sheets of newspaper and have the players stand on them instead of sitting on the chairs.

**To play**

Arrange the chairs into two parallel lines of twelve or eight, all facing forwards. Divide your group into two teams and have each team elect a leader.

Explain that the chairs/newspaper sheets represent a 'ladder' to heaven; the aim of the game is for the leaders to get their entire team up the ladder and into heaven.

Seat the opposing leaders at a table with the die and cup and a large copy of this number list:

6 = 6 forwards or 1 back
5 = move forwards 5 or split between two players (3 and 2 or 4 and 1)
4 = move 4 backwards, never forwards
3 = move 3 forwards, get another go
2 = move 2 forwards
1 = change places with another player or move 1 forward

The leaders begin by taking it in turns to throw the dice. They may place and move one player each turn, on either of the two ladders. If a player lands on a space that is already occupied, the occupant 'falls off' the ladder and has to return to the start. The player who dislodges him must say sorry – or forfeit the space himself! To reach heaven – the space on the far side of the ladder – the exact number needed must be thrown. The team members may advise their leaders on who to move and to where, but there is a maximum time limit of 30 seconds thinking time before each move is made. Keep the game moving as fast as possible.

If there are twelve players or less in the whole group, one ladder will be enough.

The first complete team to reach heaven is the winner.

**Theme points – Heaven**

Who was Jacob? What was Jacob's ladder? See Genesis 28:12. Use this game to introduce or be part of a study of this story. How do we 'get to heaven?' Jesus is 'the way to the Father'. Jesus is our ladder, there is no other way. Some of the players were 'knocked off' the ladder by rival team members: do we ever dampen or discourage people who are trying to find God? Have we ever been dampened or discouraged ourselves? We are told not to 'make our brothers stumble': we should be helping and encouraging each other. We all make mistakes and we shouldn't be afraid to say 'Sorry' to one another, and to God, from time to time. See Romans 14:13.

• **Heaven, Jacob, Jesus the way, Encouraging, Sorry**

# 69 WHERE AM I GOING?

**Equipment required**
None

**To play**
One player temporarily leaves the room. The rest agree on a 'destination' – a country or a place, eg America or the swimming pool.

The player outside then returns and, standing in the centre of the group, asks, 'Where am I going?' He points to other group members at random and they must respond by giving a clue without giving the game away. If the country was America the answers to, 'Where am I going?' could be: 'Somewhere big' or, 'Somewhere with a President.'

When the player guesses his destination, the player whose response finally gave the game away becomes the next one to go outside.

**Theme points – Heaven**
Do we know where we are going in life? Or are we just drifting? Where does God want us to go? He has a plan for our lives. We need to ask him for directions, listen to him and follow them. If you make the final 'destination' heaven you can then lead on into a discussion of how to be sure we are going there: Jesus is the way.

- **Heaven, Directions, God's plan, Jesus the way**

**Equipment needed**
A feather or two.

**To play**
Divide your group into teams of four or five. Two teams sit facing each other across the length of a table, with a feather placed in the centre. If you have a large group, have several tables and play a knock-out competition. A referee for each table would be useful!

On the signal to start, both teams try to blow the feather off the other end of the table to score a point. Everyone must remain seated! Feathers that go over the side of the table are retrieved and replaced in the centre – no one scores. Set a time limit of three to five minutes and see which team can reach the highest score in that time.

**Theme points – Holy Spirit, Wind**
If you are able to play another game with this theme (such as 'Kippers' or 'Hot air balloons') you can ask the group to tell you the common factor.

Ask if it was easy to control which way the feather blew. It probably wasn't! If someone blew the other way the feather was off again in the opposite direction. Talk about the way the wind blows. Is it always predictable? Is it always controllable? It can't be seen. No one can see your efforts at blowing the feather, but the effects can be seen and heard and felt. In what way is the wind like this? Then discuss in what ways the Holy Spirit resembles the wind. See Acts 2:2 and John 3:8.

- **Wind, Holy Spirit, Pentecost**

# 71 HOT AIR BALLOONS

**Equipment required**
One round balloon per team playing.

**To play**
Divide your group into teams, and hand each team a balloon. It helps if the balloons are different colours when you've several teams.

At the signal to start, the teams must throw their balloons into the air – and keep them there, by blowing hard! No hands are allowed! It may help to make the children clasp their hands behind their backs – or hold each other's hands in a circle. The winning team is the one whose balloon stays airborne the longest. Large teams are an advantage in this game.

You could play several rounds. The winners could be the 'best of five attempts', for example.

**Theme points – Holy Spirit, Wind**
You could bring out the point that it takes a great deal of effort to blow hard enough to keep the balloon up. But consider the power of the wind which can blow trees down etc. Go on to discuss the power of the Holy Spirit.

Pick up on the idea that the wind blows where it will, and lead into a discussion on the similarities with the Holy Spirit. See John 3:8 and Acts 2:2.

- **Holy Spirit, Wind, Pentecost**

**S T**

**Equipment required**
One simple cut-out paper fish-shape per player, magazines or sheets
of cardboard to use as fans, chalk, hoops or a travel rug to represent
the pond.

**To play**
Divide your group into teams and equip each team member with a
paper fish. Each team should be given a magazine or sheet of cardboard
with which to fan the fish and make them move along. In the centre
of your room or playing area clear a large space and either chalk a
large circle, place a large hula-hoop or put a small travel rug on the
floor. These represent the fish pond.

Up to three or four teams can play simultaneously. Make the teams
stand as far back from the pond as possible. Ten paces is ideal but
half that (or less) will do. The teams should be spread round the
circumference of the pond so that all the teams can have a member
playing at once without getting in each other's way.

On the signal to begin, one player from each team places his fish
on the ground and fans it across the intervening space and into the
pond. Fish must be completely within the circle or hoop or on to the
blanket. As soon as his fish is safely in the pond the player must rush
back and hand the fan on to the next team member. The winning team
is the first one to land all its fish in the pond. A player whose exertions
cause any fish to fly *out* of the pond must fan those fish back in – as
well as his own. Only fanning is allowed – no tricky flipping or foot
assisted shuffling please!

**Theme points – ICHTHUS/fish**
The early Christians used a fish for their secret symbol. Why? The first
letters of the Greek words Iesous CHristos THeou Uios Soter (Jesus
Christ, God's Son, Saviour) make up the word ICHTHUS – Greek for
fish.

Why did the fish move? Because the air around them moved. What
names do we have for air in motion? Wind, breeze, hurricane etc
should come up. The Holy Spirit is likened in the Bible to a wind.
How does the Holy Spirit move us? There is power in air in motion:
the Holy Spirit brings power – but what kind?

Another relevant theme is that of shared responsibility. If you fanned
someone else's fish out of the pond, you were responsible for replacing
it. We have responsibilities towards each other. We should look out
for other people's interests and not just our own. See Galatians 6:2.

- **ICHTHUS/fish, Wind, Holy Spirit, Responsibility, Fish**

# 73 KIPPERS

**Equipment required**
One old magazine per team. One cut-out newspaper fish-shape (about 30cm long and 20cm wide) per team member.

**To play**
Divide your group into teams, with a starting line on one side of the room and a finishing line on the other.

The teams line up, each player holding a 'kipper', behind the starting line. The first player in each team is given a magazine with which to fan his kipper and make it move across the room and over the finishing line. They must then run back and hand the magazine to the next team player who then fans his kipper. The first team to get all its kippers home is the winner. No kippers must be touched by hand, foot or magazine! No kipper must be moved except by fanning. Anyone seen cheating in any way must return to the start and begin again!

**Theme points – ICHTHUS/fish**
Ask if anyone can tell you who used the fish as their secret sign. The early Christians did. Does anyone know why? The word 'ICHTHUS' which means fish in Greek, also forms an acronym – each letter stands for another word, in this case Jesus Christ, God's Son, Saviour. In Greek it's Iesous CHristos THeou Uios Soter.

This game can be used in conjunction with other air-movement games such as 'Feather in the air' and 'Hot air balloons' to draw out the common theme. Ask if it was always easy to control the movement of the kippers? Some will have found it easier than others. What was moving the kippers? Air – air in motion. This is like the wind – which Jesus likened to the Holy Spirit – blowing where it will. Take it from here in a discussion of parallel images (see 'Feather in the air' game theme points). There is also power in air in motion. This is what was moving the kippers. The Holy Spirit brings power too – but what kind and how?

- **Wind, Holy Spirit, ICHTHUS/fish**

# 74 SILLY SILHOUETTES

**Equipment required**
One large-ish piece of paper for each player – wallpaper will do nicely – and a marker pen for each team, masking tape or Blu-tack. If you are able to darken the room sufficiently, you will need a powerful torch for each team – see Version A. Otherwise play Version B, which can also be played outside.

**Version A – With torches**

**To play**
The group is divided into two teams, who go to opposite sides or ends of the room so that they cannot see what the others are doing.

Each team member in turn tapes their piece of paper to the wall at head height (seated). Another team member directs the torch light on the sitter's profile while a third team member draws round the shadow on the paper. Seat the 'model' a short distance from the wall.

Take it in turns until you have a complete set of silhouettes for each team. Write the sitters' names on the backs; don't let the opposing team see these.

**Version B – Without torches**
Play as before except that the sitter will need to sit with one ear pressed to the piece of paper on the wall, while the 'artist' draws as accurately as possible round his profile. Complete the set of pictures as before with names on the backs.

Bring the two teams together again and have them sit facing each other. The team leaders take it in turns to hold up a portrait from their collection. The opposing team may then confer before being allowed one guess at who it is. At this stage just say 'Yes' or 'No' and go on to the next portrait. Keep score, and see if either team gets all the identities correct.

At the end, if you wish, they can then identify themselves and their portraits to each other.

**Theme points – images of God**
A portrait is an image. We are made in God's image: we are his creation. Point out that the images they have just made are not always recognisable: this links with the theme of flawed images. Go on to ask how God's images are spoiled: this links with themes of sin and sickness etc. See Genesis 1:26–27 and 1 Corinthians 15:49.

- **Images of God, Creation, Sin, Flawed images**

# 75 JERICHO

**Equipment required**
Hat or box (one per team) containing slips of paper with instructions on them (one per team member).

*Instructions*
Duplicate or invent new instructions so that there is one per child in the team. The instructions are:

1. Hop round Jericho on one foot
2. Run right round Jericho
3. Walk backwards round Jericho as fast as you can
4. Jump round Jericho in bunny-hops
5. Walk round Jericho heel-to-toe with each foot
6. Crawl round Jericho on your hands and knees
7. Run backwards round Jericho
8. Walk forwards round Jericho as fast as you can
9. Alternately walk three steps and then run three steps round Jericho
10. Do giant strides round Jericho

**To play**
Divide into two teams and stand in circles. Space the members an arm's length apart. In the centre of each circle place a box or hat with a set of jumbled-up instruction slips. Explain that the circles of players represent the walls of Jericho. The aim of the game is to be the first team to demolish the walls.

On the signal to start, each player in turn runs to the centre, takes an instruction slip, obeys the instructions, and returns to his place in the circle. The next player then takes his turn. As soon as everyone has had a turn and the box is empty, the walls fall down – everyone in the team sits down quickly shouting **'Crash!'** The first team to 'Crash!' wins.

If you have less than twenty people, play this as a non-team game with one circle of players. See how quickly they can bring the walls down.

**Theme points – Jericho**
How did Joshua capture Jericho? How did the teams demolish *their* walls? There were instructions that had to be obeyed (this links with the theme of obedience) even though they may have seemed a bit silly at the time. See Joshua 6:1–20.

● **Jericho, Joshua, Obeying**

# 76 CALLING OUT

**Equipment required**
None

**To play**
To make the theme point of 'being called', 'called by name' or 'called out by Jesus', play the game 'Following on' (number 51) or a similar game and have a leader positioned at the far side of the room. When everyone is engrossed in the game this leader should call out the name of one of the players and beckon him over to the other side of the room. He should explain quietly to the called-out player that he is shortly going to be used as a visual aid! Call out two or three players in this fashion and then end the game, gathering the whole group together.

**Theme points – Jesus calls us**
Ask the called-out players how they felt? Puzzled? Curious? Annoyed? Ask the other players how they felt? Curious? Indifferent? Didn't notice? Why them and not me? Now you can draw parallels with Jesus' calling of the fishermen and their reactions, and the likely reactions of those around them. See Matthew 4:18–22. Note too that the players were called out by name – so were the fishermen. Jesus knows us and calls us by name – we are all important to him. This also applies to the calling of Matthew – see Matthew 9:9.

- **Jesus calls us, Calling, Fishermen, Matthew**

# 77 ACROSS THE GAP

This game can be played indoors or outdoors. For the indoor version, the jumping will have to be done from a standing start on the edge of the string; whereas if played outdoors there can be a run-up before jumping.

**Equipment required**
Two lengths of rope or string, four chairs.

**To play**
Tie the lengths of rope or string to the bottoms of the chair legs so that you have two parallel lengths of stretched out rope. The rope should be flat on the ground. The gap between the ropes should be fairly narrow to start with – maybe a metre. The aim of the game is for the players to jump over the ropes, completely clearing the gap in the middle.

If you have a large group, you may like to divide them into two or three teams and have one member from each team run and jump simultaneously, provided the ropes are long enough. Otherwise play it as a simple turn-by-turn jump off. When everyone has jumped the original gap, move one pair of chairs and rope further away, thus widening the gap, and have a second jump off.

More and more players will be eliminated each time the gap is widened. Finally, make the gap so wide that not even your champion jumper can clear it.

**Theme points – Jesus the way**
See John 14:6, 'I am the way, the truth, and the life; no one goes to the Father except by me.' This game ties in with Jesus being the only way to the Father. We cannot reach God by our efforts alone: there is a gulf separating us from God – like the gap the children tried to jump. We can try to jump the gap by all sorts of methods (being 'good', doing 'good', saying our prayers, trying all sorts of other religions, going to church) but none of them work! We will fall in the gap (which is caused by sin) and we need Jesus to bridge the gap for us.

You can illustrate this by putting a line of chairs across your gap and saying that now anyone can cross – no need to jump – and everyone will be a winner. Through Jesus we can all 'win' the race and reach God.

- **Jesus the way, Sin**

**Equipment required**

String, sheets of newspaper or magazines. Each player needs two sheets of paper about the size of a single tabloid newspaper page.

**To play**

Divide your group into teams and line them up on one side of the room. At the signal to start, the first two players race to a finishing line marked with string along the floor. They must use their sheets of paper as stepping stones. Anyone who falls or steps off a 'stone' will fall into the river and must go back to the beginning and start again, as must anyone who tries sliding the paper along or any similar device!

When the first member has crossed the line at the far side, the next team member sets off. The first team to cross the room is the winner.

**Theme points – Jesus the way**

This is another game picking up the 'Jesus the way to the Father' theme. Ask how they got across the gap. Stepping stones and their own efforts will probably be mentioned. Ask what Jesus has to say about how we can reach God. We can only reach God through Jesus – our own efforts are useless. Ask what sort of things do we try to use as stepping stones to God. (Good works, good lives, regular church-going, other religions etc.) The trouble is that they won't work! They'll be as much use as a newspaper stepping stone across a real river. What is it that separates us from God? Not a river or string across the floor – it's sin. See John 14:6.

- **Jesus the way, Sin**

# 79 RIVER JORDAN

**Equipment required**
Heavy rubber gym mat (or row of mats), or a chalk line or line of string on the ground.

**To play**
One player is the caller; the rest of the group line up in a row behind the chalk or string line or on the edge of the mat(s). Explain that the mats (or one side of the line) represent the river bank and the space in front represents the river.

The caller now issues a series of instructions. He calls: 'On the banks!' 'In the river!' On the banks!' in quick succession. The players must jump in the river or on to the banks as directed and as fast as possible.

The caller will occasionally shout: 'On the river!' or, 'In the banks!' If anyone makes a move on these calls they are deemed to have fallen in the river and are washed away – out of the game for this round.

The last player in becomes the caller for the next round.

**Theme points – John the Baptist**
As an introduction to John the Baptist baptising in the River Jordan, ask who can tell you what happened 'in the river' and 'on the banks' and who was there? See Luke 3:1–18. Or use the game as an illustration of the need to keep on listening carefully to what is being said and not just following the crowd (This link with themes of listening to God/Jesus, obeying.)

- **John the Baptist, Listening, Obeying**

# 80 SNATCH!

**Equipment required**
Prepare a trayful of objects. These should be:

a. Small, wrapped sweets (enough for all)
b. One Mars bar
c. Some screwed up empty toffee wrappers
d. A safety pin
e. A rubber
f. A pencil
g. A piece of Blu-tack or Plasticine with a £1 coin concealed inside it

**To play**
Put the covered tray on a table, have everyone gather round, and announce that when you uncover the tray and shout 'Snatch!' everyone is to grab one object – which they can keep!

**Theme points – Judgment**
How do we make our judgments about people, about objects, about values? In theory everyone will try to grab the Mars bar and, failing that, a toffee; at which point you reveal the £1 in the Blu-tack. If someone has grabbed the Blu-tack you can still make your point, but it might cost you £1!

Point out that God judges us by what's inside not outside. We should not judge others by appearances. See Hebrews 4:12, 13.

• **Judgment, Appearances**

**Equipment required**
Recorded music.

**To play**
When the music plays everyone parades or dances round the room. When it stops, the leader shouts a number. The entire group must form clumps of players with that number in the clump.

Count your players before you start, and if necessary incorporate a leader or two to make up a number that divides easily into several other numbers, eg 28 which is divisible by 14, 7, 4, and 2.

Begin by calling the number of players present to get one large clump. Then call the numbers that divide into it exactly – so that to begin with everyone 'belongs'. Now explain that the game is hotting up – it starts getting tricky – and the next number won't fit. Anyone outside a clump will be out. Call numbers that don't divide exactly and progress down to the last two or three players left in. Then call your original total group number for your very last round!

**Theme points – Kingdom of God**
The very first and last clumps had room for everyone. The Kingdom of God is like this.

How did it feel to be left out of a clump? Not much fun. We should be aware of the feelings of outsiders. The church is not an exclusive club: we should be trying to get everyone to join in and be part of our 'clump' – the Kingdom of God. This is what evangelism is all about. That's why you ended with a clump of everyone together. And there is no need to try to force your way in – Jesus will never turn anyone away. See John 6:37.

- **Kingdom of God, Room for all, Outsiders, Evangelism, Church/family**

# 82 KING MAKING

**Equipment required**
A piece of chalk, a packet of brightly coloured sticky labels – the larger the better.

**To play**
Divide your room or playing area into three recognisable sections, with two small home bases either side of a large 'kingdom'. One player begins the game as King Maker and is handed the chalk. He puts a sticky label on his clothes.

All the players except the King Maker assemble in one of the home areas. Tell them that the King rules over the central area – the kingdom – but he's all alone and wants others to join him. But to do this he's got to put his mark on them to make them like him – only kings can live in the kingdom! When he calls, '1–2–3–Go!' all the players must dash across the kingdom and try to reach the other home base without being marked with the chalk. The King Maker must call, '1–2–3–King!' each time he chalks someone. Any chalked player must stick a label on their clothes and remain in the kingdom for the next round. After the first round, any players who are now kings can help stick labels on those who get chalked next time. They can also help the King Maker by linking hands and trying to direct running players towards the King Maker – although they must not touch them or restrain them in any way.

To start a second round the King Maker calls, '1–2–3–Go!' again and the remaining unmarked players rush across to the other home base.

Continue until the last player is 'crowned' and then play again, if you wish, with that player as the new King Maker.

**Theme points – Kingdom of God**
Who is the 'King' of the 'Kingdom of God'? It's Jesus. How does he mark us out as his? By baptism with water. 'Whoever believes and is baptized will be saved,' reads Mark 16:16. We are also 'labelled' or 'sealed' by the Holy Spirit. Ephesians 1:13 reads, 'God put his stamp of ownership on you by giving you the Holy Spirit he had promised.' Those who had been made 'kings' helped to turn the escaping players towards the King Maker. How do we turn other people towards Jesus so that he can make them his own as well? By evangelism and witnessing. Jesus makes us members of his kingdom to reign with him!

The theme of kings and kingdoms here could also be used as a very basic introduction to a study of King David or King Solomon.

- **Kingdom of God, Baptism, Evangelism, Witnessing, Sealed with the Spirit, David, Solomon**

# 83 ISLANDS

**Equipment required**
Oddments of carpet or small mats (eg bath mats); one per team. For a team of ten members the pieces/mats should measure about 50×75cm.

**To play**
Divide your group into teams. Explain that there are sharks in the sea, but fortunately there are a few islands as well. Point to the mats.

**Either** give the signal to start, and the first team to get all its members on to their island – no feet in the water – wins.

**Or** play for a set time limit (eg sixty seconds) and any team members not on an island are deemed to have been eaten by the sharks. The team with most members surviving wins.

If there's a draw you could cut a piece off each carpet oddment and have a replay!

**Theme points – Lifestyle/Christian life**
There wasn't a lot of room for everyone on the mats. Some had to balance on one foot and hang on to everyone else: some had a toe-hold, others were well in. What is your Christian life like – are you well in or are you hanging on by a toe-hold and depending on others to keep you in? Or are you struggling to get aboard at all? Players could identify themselves with these positions. Also, on a 'kingdom' theme, there wasn't really room for everyone on the islands – but God has promised that there is room for everyone in the Kingdom of Heaven. And on a Christmas theme: there was no room for Jesus when he came into the world – he was born in a stable. Is there room for Jesus in our lives or have we pushed him out today, too? How do we 'make room' for Jesus?

- **Lifestyle/Christian life, Room for all, Room for Jesus**

# 84 THE ADMIRAL'S ABOARD

**Equipment required**
List of instructions written on a piece of paper. Possible instructions are:

a. Port! (Meaning: *run to left-hand wall*)
b. Starboard! (*Run to right-hand wall*)
c. Fore! (*Run to front*)
d. Aft! (*Run to back*)
e. Climb the rigging! (*On the spot; rope climbing actions*)
f. Swab the decks! (*Mopping actions*)
g. Cannon-ball coming! (*Lie flat on the floor*)
h. Admiral's aboard (*Stop dead, stand straight and salute at attention*)

**To play**
Explain to the group that they are all sailors on a ship. The captain is expecting a visit from the admiral. Read out the instructions before you begin and make sure everyone understands what to do when each is called.

One player is chosen as the captain and is given the list of instructions from which he can call at random. The captain commences calling, but when he calls, 'Admiral's aboard!' the last person to obey is out. Play on until all but one are eliminated. That player becomes the next captain.

To lessen the sting of being caught out, use these players as referees. Tell them you need help to spot who's out next, giving them a continuing active role in the game.

**Theme points – Listening**
Ask the group what were the keys to winning? The following points should come up:

*Listening* Success in the game depends on listening carefully – every time. So it is with listening to God.

*Obeying* Success also depends on instant obedience to the captain's commands – and with obeying God's commands.

*Authority* The captain is in charge; he has authority over the sailors, who must do as he says. He in turn is under the authority of the admiral. Bring this point out by playing this game in succession with 'The sergeant says' and ask the group to tell you what the games have in common. Jesus has this authority. See Matthew 28:18.

*Readiness* Success in this game depends on being ready for the admiral to come aboard without warning at any moment. Are we ready for Jesus to return?

- **Listening, Obeying, Authority, Readiness, Jesus' return**

# 85 THE SERGEANT SAYS

**Equipment required**
List of actions written on a piece of paper. These actions are:

a. Attention!
b. Salute!
c. Slope arms!
d. Open fire!
e. At ease!
f. Quick march! (*on the spot*)
g. Slow march! (*on the spot*)

**To play**
Read through the actions and ensure everyone understands their meaning. Choose a sergeant and give him the list.

Play begins as in 'Simon says', with the sergeant giving orders from the list. They must only be obeyed when prefaced by the words, 'The sergeant says.'

Either play an elimination game or allow the first player to make a mistake to become the new sergeant.

**Theme points – Listening**
The children had to listen carefully and not just copy their neighbours. We must listen to God for ourselves and not just copy other people.

The theme of obedience is also relevant: we should be doing only what 'the sergeant says', which is not necessarily what others may try to tell us.

● **Listening, Obeying**

# 86 TWIRLING

### Equipment required
Fairly large metal or plastic plate or tray – anything unbreakable that will spin for a while when placed on the floor and given a twirl.

### To play
Everyone sits round in a large circle. This game really needs everyone to know everyone else's name. If this is not possible, number all the players off round the circle. They keep their number throughout the game. Make sure they know their own number – get them to call them out round the circle before you start. One player is chosen to be 'It'. He goes to the centre of the circle, spins the plate, and simultaneously shouts either a name or a number. The player whose name or number is called must leap up, run to the centre of the circle and grab the plate before it stops spinning. If he fails, he becomes 'It' for the next turn. If he succeeds, 'It' has to try again to catch someone unawares.

### Theme points – Listening
What were the keys to success in this game? Listening and being ready if you were called. We need to listen if we want to hear God speak to us. Also, on the theme of being called, we are 'called out' by 'It'. As Christians we are 'called out' by Jesus. How do we hear and respond to Jesus' calling? In the game we were called by another player. We can hear Jesus' calling through other people. This can be evangelism/ witnessing. 'Holiness' means being 'set apart' or 'called out'. We are told to be a 'holy people' – called out by God. See Isaiah 62:12, 'You will be called "God's Holy People, the People the LORD Has Saved." '

- **Listening, Hearing, Obeying, Readiness, Evangelism, Holiness, Jesus calls us**

# 87 WHAT AM I SHOUTING?

**Equipment required**
A list of proverbs written on a sheet of paper. Possible proverbs are:

A stitch in time saves nine.
Every cloud has a silver lining.
Too many cooks spoil the broth.
Marry in haste; repent at leisure.
More haste, less speed.
Spare the rod and spoil the child.
He who laughs last laughs longest.
Many a true word is spoken in jest.

**To play**
Divide the group into two teams to sit facing each other. Assign a proverb to each team; assign one word of each proverb to each team member. Two members can share a word if necessary.

On a count of three the first team shout their words simultaneously. The second team has to guess what they were shouting. Then the second team shout their proverb and the first team tries to guess what it was.

This can go on for as long as you like, with the teams scoring points for correct guesses.

TV programme titles, song titles, etc can all be used – or Bible verses.

**Theme points – Hearing/listening**
Ask the children to tell you why it was hard to hear what the phrase was that was being shouted. It was because too many voices were being heard at once. Hearing God speak/listening to him needs a quiet time so that his voice is not drowned out by others. How can the children make room in their lives for a quiet listening time?

● **Hearing, Listening, Discernment, Quiet time**

# 88 WATER BOMBS

**Equipment required**
Two balloons half-filled with water; recorded music.

**To play**
The children stand round in a circle at arm's length apart. When the music starts the balloons must be thrown from player to player – as in pass the parcel.

When the music stops, whoever is holding a balloon is out. Anyone who throws a balloon that bursts is out. Everyone steps back one pace each time the music stops. Use only one balloon if the group is small.

**Theme points – Living water**
With all the frantic activity and exploding balloons, this game is like playing with 'living' water – with a life of its own! See John 4:1–14 and John 7:37–38.

What did Jesus mean when he talked about 'living water'? What is it, where does it come from? Take your study from here.

- **Living water, Holy Spirit**

# 89 THE LOST SHEEP

**Equipment required**
None

**To play**
Begin with the whole group standing in a circle, facing outwards, with one player, the shepherd, standing in the centre.

The shepherd says, 'I've lost a sheep!' and taps a player on the shoulder. The player must say, 'What does he look like?' The shepherd then begins to describe another player, eg 'He's wearing jeans,' or, 'He's got a blue shirt,' etc until the player can recognise the description from memory and shout: 'That's Joe!' (or whoever).

The named player then runs round the outside of the circle with the first player in pursuit. He must try to get back to his place in the circle without being tagged by the player who named him. If he succeeds, he becomes the next shepherd. If he fails, the first player becomes shepherd. The original shepherd rejoins the circle.

*Note*: Players can run either way round the circle, but once the chase has started they must keep going and not turn round half-way.

**Theme points – Lost sheep**
See particularly Matthew 18:12–14, Luke 15:4–7, 1 Peter 2:25 and John 10:1–16. We are like sheep that have gone astray and Jesus is the good shepherd.

There are many sheep/shepherd references in the Bible: use this game as an introduction to them and that theme. Point out that as a shepherd knows his sheep well, so Jesus, the good shepherd, knows everything about us, and not just a superficial description of our outward appearances.

Who are the lost sheep of today? They are not just the obvious ones (eg criminals, drug addicts etc). Anyone who does not know Jesus as Lord is a lost sheep. Jesus is looking for them and calling their names – like the shepherd in the game!

• **Lost sheep, The good shepherd, Jesus knows us**

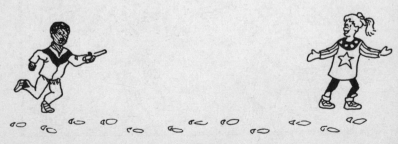

# 90 SHEEP IN THE MUD

**Equipment required**
None

**To play**
One or more players are chosen to be sheep-dogs. For a short game two sheep-dogs per twelve players is about right.

On the word, 'Go!' the sheep disperse and the dog(s) pursue them and try to tag them. Tagged sheep must stand still with legs apart and 'baa' loudly. The dog(s) must bark! Tagged sheep may be released by a free sheep crawling under their legs.

The game ends when all the sheep have been rounded up and are static – and bleating!

**Theme points – Lost sheep**
This game ties in neatly with the parable of the lost sheep (Luke 15:1–7). You can start by asking why it is important for lost sheep to be quickly rounded up and about the dangers they may encounter, and take it from there.

You could also use this as a starter for a discussion of the good shepherd – John 10:11–16.

- **Lost sheep, Seeking, Saving, The good shepherd**

# 91 STREAMS AND RIVERS

**Equipment required**
None

**To play**
Explain that one player is going to be a 'pike' and another a 'minnow'. We all know that pikes chase minnows in order to eat them!

The rest of the players stand in straight lines and rows, at arm's length apart in any direction. They should be able to touch fingertips with the next person in line either side of them or, by turning a quarter-turn, in front and behind them. They look like this:

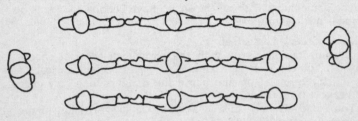

The instruction, 'Streams!' means 'face the leader'. The children's outstretched arms will make channels. The instruction 'Rivers!' means 'turn a quarter-turn'. The children's arms will now make channels at right angles to the original streams. The leader begins by calling, 'Streams!' and, 'Rivers!' a couple of times so that the players can practise turning swiftly from one to the other.

The pike must chase the minnow and try to tag him. He may only chase up and down the rows of players.

Meanwhile, the leader may call, 'Streams!' or, 'Rivers!' as required, to change the layout and give the minnow an avenue of escape. Neither pike nor minnow may break through a line and no tagging across a line is allowed.

The game really needs a minimum of eleven players – a pike and a minnow, plus three rows of three players.

When the minnow is caught, another two players swap places with the pike and minnow.

**Theme points – Moses/Red Sea**
Just when the minnow thought all was lost – the waters parted and an escape was possible. Use this as a parallel/introduction to the Israelites crossing of the Red Sea. Who commanded the waters to part in the game/the Bible story? See Exodus 14.

You could also pick up on the theme of 'making the way straight' and John the Baptist's message. The leader in the game was making a straight path for the minnow. John the Baptist cried: 'Make straight the way of the Lord.' What does this mean? See Luke 3:1–18.

• **Moses/Red Sea, John the Baptist**

# 92 WHOSE ZOO?

**Equipment required**
Pen and paper for each team.

**To play**
Divide the group into two teams; size doesn't really matter much. Send the teams to opposite ends of the room, out of earshot of each other.

Tell them that every member of each team is to choose the identity of a different animal or bird, the team leader should list these on the paper provided.

When every team member has made their choice, and the lists are compiled, explain that when you give the signal everyone in both teams must, as loudly as possible, make the noise appropriate to their own particular bird or animal! The signal will be a dropped hand. When you raise it again they must stop – instantly!

Give the signal and allow five seconds of unabated din; then stop. Explain that they must now write down – or tell their leaders to write down – as many birds and animals as possible that they think they can identify from the opposing team. Give another five seconds of cacophony for them to be listening as well as yodelling, if you wish.

When the teams have compiled the lists, get a member of one team to read the list of creatures they think they heard. Check this with the list held by the opposing team. Score a point for every correctly identified creature. Repeat the process with the other team.

Did any of the team have the same birds and animals? Call up the pairs you have found in this way and get them to make their noises together.

**Theme points – Noah's ark**
Either use this as an introduction to the story of Noah (Who collected two of every creature?) or use it as a spot of light relief in the middle of a Noah Bible study. Point out that the Ark must have sounded a bit like this! Most people know the Noah's ark story – but how many know the bits before and after the incident of the animals' collection? Either get someone to tell you or start your study here. See Genesis 6:9, 9:17.

• **Noah's ark, Flood**

# 93 ALL TIED UP!

**Equipment required**
Two lengths of strong rope, beach ball or sponge football. Four chairs.

**To play**

*Game A – Football*
Divide the group into two teams and have them stand close together while you rope them up into a fairly closely tied bunch – the rope must not slip down when they (attempt!) to move. Be careful not to hurt anyone and ensure that no one gets squashed too badly in the centre of the bunch. Put two chairs, spaced apart, at each end of the room for goals. Play 'football' for three minutes each way.

*Game B – Stampede*
Rope the teams together as before but this time at the word, 'Go!' they simply race to the far side of the room, round a chair and back to base.

**Theme points – One body/many parts**
Point out that just as the teams were 'all tied up', the Bible tells us that we are one body of Christians, joined together not by rope but by the Holy Spirit. To get anywhere co-operation is necessary. The Bible tells us that because we are joined together when one part suffers, all suffer. Certainly this is true in the game, where success lies in everyone pacing themselves to suit everyone, not just the most agile. See 1 Corinthians 12:26.

You could play this game alongside game 94 and ask what was the common denominator (it's being 'joined together') and proceed from there.

- **One body/many parts, One body/one Spirit, Joined together, Co-operation**

# 94 ALL SEWN UP!

**Equipment required**
One teaspoon and one ball of string per team. For a really exciting version put the spoons into the freezer until just before you play!

**To play**
Tie a loose end from the ball of string securely round the 'necks' of the spoons. Divide the group into two teams – standing in line. It doesn't matter how large the teams are in this game. Hand the front player of each team a ball of string with spoon attached. On the word 'Go' they must thread the spoon down the necks of their shirts and out of the legs of their trousers at the bottom, unravelling the string as they go. The spoon is then passed to the next person in line, who does the same – and so on until the whole group is 'all sewn up'. You can then play a second round of the game, if you wish, with the groups competing to be the first to reverse the whole process and end up with a ball of string as they started.

### Theme points – One body/one Spirit
See Colossians 2:19 and Ephesians 4:16. Point out that the winning team was 'all sewn up' – joined together. What was joining them? String! The Bible tells us that as Christians we are one body – joined together not by string but by the Holy Spirit!

• **One body/one Spirit, Joined together**


# 95 LINK-UPS

**Equipment required**
None

**To play**
The children form pairs, back-to-back. They link arms at the elbows in this position. On the command, 'Sit!' all the pairs must sit down and then stand up again.

Now they form fours and repeat the sit/stand, form fours to make eights, and so on, until the whole group is linked up in a big circle and try doing the **sit** together.

### Theme points – Peace
Romans 12:18 reads, 'Do everything possible on your part to live in peace with everybody.' The final mass link-up was only possible because everyone was trying to make it work. It began with pairs trying to work together and grew from there. It's like this when we want everyone to live in peace. It's got to begin in a small way with individuals and their neighbours – and grow from there.

• **Peace, Harmony, Working together**

# 96 ALLELUIA! AMEN!

**Equipment required**
None

**To play**
All the players sit in a circle. One player is 'It'. 'It' commences play by pointing to any player and saying any one of the following:

| | | | | |
|---|---|---|---|---|
| a. | Alleluia! | > The response | > | Amen! |
| b. | Amen! | > must be | > | Alleluia! |
| c. | Allelu-Amen! | > instant | > | Amen-Allelu! |
| d. | Amen-Allelu! | > and like this | > | Allelu-Amen! |

Any player 'It' points at must jump to their feet and make the appropriate response before sitting down again.

Play continues in quick-fire fashion until someone slips up and makes the wrong response. They then become 'It'.

**Theme points – Praise**
Ask if anyone can tell you the meaning of 'Alleluia' and 'Amen'. 'Alleluia' means 'Praise the Lord' and 'Amen' means 'I agree' or 'So be it'. Point out that the children have just spent the last five minutes or so 'rejoicing in the Lord'. We are told to praise the Lord at all times. See Philippians 4:4.

You could also link the leaping up and shouting the responses with the story of the healing of the lame man in Acts 3:1–10.

• **Praise, Rejoicing**


# 97 FIREMEN   &#9411;

**Equipment required**
Small slips of paper – three for each group of three players. Larger (A4) sheets of paper and pen, one for each group of players.

**To play**
Divide your group into sub-groups of three. If you have an odd player or two left over then either co-opt a leader into making up a threesome or tag a spare player on to a group and make one group a foursome. Give that group one extra small slip of paper.

Ensure, as far as you are able, that there is at least one player in each group with no literacy problems.

Tell them that they are all firefighters compiling a report; their houses have caught fire, and they're giving an account of what was saved and why. Each group should select a secretary to write the report – this player is given the large sheet of paper and the slips. At the top of the large sheet of paper he should write: 'Our house caught fire, this is what we saved and why,' and write the numbers 1, 2, 3 down the side of the sheet.

Now they must decide on three things they would save – each group member must choose one item. The secretary writes these items down on the individual slips of paper – one per slip. Then he must write a reason for saving each object against the numbers 1, 2 and 3, but not the name of the object. So a group might write:

Our house caught fire, this is what we saved and why

| My dog | 1. Because it's good company |
| My bike | 2. Because I ride it to school |
| My computer | 3. Because it has got all my course-work on it |

Now the fun starts! All the individual slips of paper are put in a box and shaken up so that they are well mixed. In turn, a member of each group dips in the box, takes a slip at random and says, 'Our house caught fire, this is what we saved and why'. He then reads the name of the object – and the secretary reads the first reason on the list! When all the groups have read their first object and reason the action is repeated with another group member taking a second 'object' out of the box and the secretaries reading the second reason and so on. If you have a fourth member to one team, he takes the last slip and his group secretary reads out the reason for saving it.

### Theme points – Priorities
Obviously the objects and reasons won't match very well. Some mismatches will be funnier than others.

How did the children make their choice of objects? They will already have had some discussion between themselves, ask them to share some of their ideas. How do they decide what is most important to them in life? How do we make decisions? Colossians 3:15 shows that the peace that Christ gives is to guide us in the decisions we make. How do we find this peace in our decision making? What should our priorities be in life?

● **Priorities, Choices, Decisions, Peace**

# 98 THEN THE BOILER BURST!

**Equipment required**
Slips of paper with story titles written on them, hat, box or any other suitable container.

**To play**
All the children sit round in a circle. One is chosen as story-teller. The story can be as long or as short as you wish, but should end suddenly with the phrase 'and then the boiler burst.' At this point all the group must dash for a pre-arranged 'home' – last one in becomes the next story-teller.

It may help to have a selection of story titles on pieces of paper. Each story-teller takes one out of the hat before commencing their tale and bases their 'ripping yarn' on these suggested titles:

| | |
|---|---|
| Goldilocks | Shipwrecked |
| Three little pigs | Earthquake |
| Chicken Little | Sleeping Beauty |
| Red Riding Hood | Cinderella |

*Sample game*
The storyteller picks 'Goldilocks' out of the hat and begins:

'One upon a time, um, there was a girl with all this hair, um, blonde, and her name was, er, Goldilocks, and she went off into the woods and found a cottage and went in and – then the boiler burst!

**Theme points – Readiness**
Tell the group that Jesus is coming again, just as unexpectedly as the end of the story. Were they ready for the 'boiler burst'? Will they be ready for Jesus when he comes? Some people are better prepared than others. How can we be better prepared?

• **Readiness, Jesus' return**

**Equipment required**
Old newspapers and magazines, staplers, sticky tape, string.

**To play**
Divide your group into small teams of three to five players. Give each team a pile of newspapers, tape, stapler, string.

Tell them that one of their group has been invited to a wedding and has nothing to wear! They have five or ten minutes to create a suit: jacket and trousers or 'posh frock' for him or her to wear. Hats are optional! They must choose a 'wedding guest' from their members and the rest set to to create a masterpiece. At the end of your chosen time limit, have a fashion parade! Anyone whose garments disintegrate is disqualified. Select the winner by popular acclaim.

**Theme points – Readiness**
These wedding guests were caught on the hop – they hadn't a thing to wear! Will we be ready for Jesus when he comes again? See Matthew 22:1–14.

How was the winner chosen? By appearances. God does not judge by appearances. He sees into our hearts and sees us as we really are. We should not judge by appearances either!

Paper clothes are not much use to anyone except for a laugh. The Bible tells us to wear the 'armour of God'. What is this? We are also told to be 'clothed in righteousness'. What does this mean? These wedding guests weren't ready to respond to the 'invitation'. Are we ready to respond to Jesus' invitation? Why do people refuse invitations? What excuses do they make? Why do people turn down Jesus' invitation?

* **Readiness, Appearances, Jesus' return, Armour of God, Clothed in righteousness, Invitations**

### Equipment required
Dice and throwing cup for each team participating. Ball of string and scissors for each team.

### To play
Divide the group into teams and get each team to choose a volunteer to be tied up. Put a chair for each of the volunteers on the far side of the room. Now get the teams to tie them using simple knots and bows so that they are easy to remove. It is important that all volunteers are tied up in the same way, following these instructions:

a.  Cut a length of string and tie the wrists together.
b.  Now do the same to the ankles.
c.  Now cut a length and tie the legs to the chair legs.
d.  Now tie a length round the waist to the chair back.
e.  Now tie the arms (wrists being already tied) to the laps and under the chair seat.

When this has been done, the teams retire to the other side of the room. On the signal to start, they begin to throw the dice in turn. Any team member who throws a six may run, untie and remove one piece of string. Play is suspended until that team member is back in the group with the string – they then continue. The winning team is the first to free their captive member – who runs back to team base for them to win.

### Theme points – Release/captives
The game centres on someone who is first of all tied up and unable to move and is then released. What kind of things tie us up and prevent us from being effective Christians? Who can set us free? It's Jesus.

• **Release/captives, Sin**

# 101 TURNAROUND

**Equipment required**
Soft ball for each team playing.

**To play**
Divide your groups into teams. Each team should choose a bowler. The rest of the team members are the skittles. The skittles should line up in rows at one side of the room or playing space. There should be a gap between the teams, but the team members themselves should stand close to each other in a row – and face the wall. Mark 'bowling spots' on the other side of the room: a mark on the floor or a line of string. The bowlers may only bowl from their spots or from behind the string.

Explain that the bowlers have to bowl their balls and touch their team members on the legs with the ball. If a bowler achieves a 'strike', that team member turns around. Bowling continues until the entire team is facing the bowler. The first team to achieve a complete turn-around is the winner. If a ball strikes the legs of a player who is already turned around then he must turn again and face the wall. Any player who is struck anywhere other than on the legs must face the wall. The bowlers themselves must face away from their teams and bowl by means of bending over and rolling the ball between their feet.

Either allow the team members to retrieve and throw the balls to the bowlers, or have leaders or team members as ballboys. It's best if the bowlers remain in their bowling positions to avoid the temptation of bowling other than in the permitted manner.

**Theme points – Repentance**
The aim of the game was to achieve a complete 'turnaround' of the whole team. Repentance is all about turning around. What do we turn away from when we repent? Who do we turn towards? How can we do this – and stay turned around? Go on from here. Discuss Bible characters who repented (eg Mary Magdalene, Jonah, the woman at the well, St Paul etc).

• **Repentance, Sinners, Sorry**

# 102 DODGEM

**Equipment required**
Foam tennis ball or sock ball.

**To play**
Divide the group into two teams – you need at least six members in each team. One team forms a circle, fairly well spaced out, the other team members stand in the centre of the circle. The outer circle players must stand still at all times; the inner players are free to move.

The aim of the game is for the circle team to throw the ball backwards and forwards to each other and try to hit members of the opposing team on the legs, below the knees, in the process. The 'target' team may dodge about at will within the circle and may use clenched fists to repel the ball. Any player who is hit on the legs must leave the circle. Play for a few minutes and then change the teams over. The winning team is the one with the most surviving players at the end of the time limit.

**Theme points – Responsibility**
Keys to success for the target team were evasion and dodging successfully. What do we try to avoid in life? some things we *should* avoid – trouble is one of them! Use this point to discuss whatever your topic for avoidance might be. Alternatively, we sometimes try to dodge our responsibilities. We 'don't want to be bothered.' Jesus was never too busy to care. God always 'bothers'. What do we try to 'dodge'?

• **Responsibility, Sharing burdens**

116

# 103 PASSING THE BUCK

**Equipment required**
One or two tennis balls or foam footballs.

**To play**
The team forms a circle of players with 'It' in the centre. If the group is very large have two balls passing round – and possibly two players as 'It' if the game proves too difficult.

The ball is passed and thrown round the circle as fast as possible. 'It' must try to tag whoever is holding the ball. If a player throws a ball so wildly that no one can catch it or if he is tagged holding the ball he becomes 'It'.

**Theme points – Responsibility**
This game involves passing the ball on as quickly as possible. We do this with responsibilities sometimes – this is called 'passing the buck'. Jesus did not do this. He took responsibility for us and for our sins on the cross. He taught the disciples not to 'pass the buck'. Feeding the hungry; healing; preaching – we are to take on the responsibility of acting for Jesus, and not just evade difficulties and pass them on fast to someone else.

- **Responsibility, Cross**

# 104 CHANGEOVER

**Equipment required**
Empty bottle.

**To play**
All the players except one should be sitting in a circle. The player in the centre spins the bottle. When the bottle stops, the players opposite each end of the bottle must change places. The middle player tries to sit in a vacant place.

**Theme points – Room for all**
The player in the middle had no place in the circle – he was an outsider and had to force a way in. John 14:2 tells us that there is room for everyone in the Kingdom of God – and no need to force a way in because Jesus is the 'way in'. John 14:6 reads, 'I am the way, the truth, and the life; no one goes to the Father except by me.'

- **Room for all, Kingdom of God, Jesus the way**

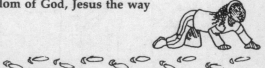

# 105 OUTSIDER TAG

**Equipment required**
None

**To play**
The group stand in a circle, facing inwards with their hands clasped behind their backs. One player is chosen as the 'outsider' and must stand outside the circle.

Play begins as the outsider walks or runs round the circle and taps the clasped hands of one of the players.

The tagged player must now race round the outside of the circle in the opposite direction to the outsider, who likewise races round the circle and tries to occupy the vacant place.

Whoever reaches the space first claims it and the remaining player becomes the outsider for the next round.

**Theme points – Room for all**
There is room for everyone in the Kingdom of Heaven – there is no need to force a way in. See John 14:2.

How does it feel to be an 'outsider'? Jesus came to 'seek and save the lost' – the outsiders were the ones he cared about most. See Luke 19:10.

• **Room for all, Outsiders**

**Equipment required**
None

**To play**
This is simply a game of tag with one person as 'It' and tagged players either being out or joining 'It' in chasing other players. The difference is that when closely pursued, they can claim temporary immunity by performing a pre-arranged action (eg sitting down, hugging another player, standing on one foot with hands on head etc). If they claim 'immunity' they must immediately start counting aloud to ten. They must get up and go again as soon as they finish counting – or be tagged.

**Theme points – Salvation**
Immunity is a kind of safety. Jesus give us 'immunity' from sin and death. Unlike this game, however, our salvation or safety does not evaporate after ten seconds! Jesus says he will never turn anyone away who comes to him – there is complete security with Jesus. See Hebrews 13:5: 'God has said, "I will never leave you; I will never abandon you." '

• **Salvation, Security, Safety, Sin**

# 107 WHIZZ QUIZ

**Equipment required**
Set of quiz questions for each team playing. Make these up yourself or use a quiz book. They can be Bible, general knowledge or trivia questions. Make sure there is a wide range so that every child will be able to get one right.

**To play**
Two leaders with sets of questions stand in two corners of the room.

Divide the group into two teams and tell them that they are going to jail and can only be bailed out if someone can answer a question correctly on their behalf. Now make the two teams go and stand in the other two corners of the room. The teams each send a volunteer to their quiz-master who asks them an (easy) question. When they get it right (keep asking questions until they get one right) they can run and grab a captive team member and bring them back. They are now asked another question. When one of them gets it right, they both run, still holding hands and grab another captive. Play continues like this until one team has released all its captives.

**Theme points – Salvation**
How were the captives released from jail? Someone 'answered' for them. Jesus 'answered' for us – he took our place on the Cross. As a result, if we take his hand, he sets us free from sin and death. See Acts 4:12, 'Salvation is to be found through him alone.'

At the end of the game the whole team were released – but it was a *chain* reaction beginning with one person who helped free another, and then another. If we are set free by Jesus we can help others find freedom too, and they in turn can tell others. This is what Jesus told us to do: to share the Good News!

- **Salvation, Captivity/sin, Evangelism, Good news, Cross**

This is basically the same as 'What's my line?' except that you choose occupations that all have your theme word in common (eg 'saving').

**Equipment required**
Write these occupations on five slips of paper:

Stamp collector
Life-guard
Bank manager
Goal keeper
Time and motion expert

**To play**
Five children perform, in turn, a brief mime of the occupation on their slip. The others try to guess what they are, by asking ten questions, which may only be answered 'Yes' or 'No'.

As each occupation is revealed write the answers up where they can be seen.

**Theme points – Saviour**
When all five occupations have been discovered ask what they all have in common: they all save something or someone – stamps, people, money, goals, time. Ask if anyone can think of any other kind of saving. Children may mention saving grace, or that Jesus saves people. Lead into your theme of saviour/saving.

• **Saviour**

# 109 CAVEMEN

**Equipment required**
None

**To play**
Some of the group form pairs and put their arms up and hands together to make an arch – these are the caves. The rest of the players are cavemen – except for one, who is the dinosaur. The cavemen all take refuge from the dinosaur inside a cave.

On the shout of, 'Change!' all the cavemen must run to another cave. The dinosaur tries to tag them. Tagged players become dinosaurs.

The last player in starts the next round as the first dinosaur. Let everyone have a go at being a caveman!

**Theme points – Security**
Safety in this game is found in the caves. We find ours in Jesus and we don't have to leave our security behind us when we step out into the world, either! Deuteronomy 33:27 reads, 'God has always been your defence; his eternal arms are your support.'

- **Saviour, Security, Safety**

# 110  SHARKS IN THE SEA

**Equipment required**
Hoops, sheets of newspaper, or chairs – enough for about a third of the players. The hoops should be dotted around the room as islands.

**To play**
One player is the shark. The swimmers may find safety on an island. Any swimmer can claim an island. If it is occupied, the occupant must leave immediately when challenged.

The shark tries to tag the swimmers: if tagged, they become sharks as well. As the number of 'swimmers' decreases remove a few islands to keep the game moving, or introduce a time limit of thirty seconds for staying on any one island.

The last player in starts next round as the first shark.

**Theme points – Security**
Safety in this game is on the islands where the sharks can't reach you. Our security is in Jesus – and nobody can remove that safety (unlike in the game). See Romans 8:38–39: 'Nothing can separate us from God's love.'

- **Security, Saviour, Safety**

# 111  HUNT THE COIN  **T**

**Equipment required**
You will need a coin, to be hidden.

**To play**
One player leaves the room or is blindfolded and stands in a corner. The remaining players hide the coin.

Everyone sits round in a circle and the chosen player returns to the room or removes blindfold. He now has to find the coin. The other players start to sing or hum a simple repetitive chorus such as 'Praise God from whom all blessings flow', varying the volume from very quiet to very loud depending on how close the seeker is to success.

When the coin is found, someone else is chosen to be the seeker and the game recommences.

**Theme points – Seeking**
This game ties in with the parable of the 'lost coin' (Luke 15:8–10), particularly in the link with 'rejoicing' when the coin is found, when the chorus humming was loudest! It can also be used to introduce the theme of seeking or saving.

- **Seeking, Saving, Lost coin, Lost people**

This is an acting game with many applications. The theme here is 'service' but other themes could be substituted and the actions modified to fit.

**Equipment required**
Slips of paper with the following written on them:

Tennis stars practising their service
Self-service in a supermarket
A butler serving drinks to M'Lord
Dinner ladies serving lunch
SAS men storming a building

**To play**
Allocate the slips to the children. They can share slips as necessary but they should not let any of the others know what is on their slip. They must take it in turns to act out what was on their slip. The others must guess what they were doing.

When all the slips have been guessed, ask the group what was the common denominator. The word 'service' should emerge.

**Theme points – Service**
Point out that Jesus wants us to 'serve' one another, but in a different way from any of the 'service' mimed. Go on to find out what Jesus meant by 'service'.

*Other applications*
*Good News* – Have scenes of watching TV, opening a letter, reading a newspaper, listening to someone talking etc.
*Saving* – Have scenes of stamp collecting, goal keeping, putting money in a piggy bank, life-guard in a swimming pool etc.
*Authority* – Have scenes involving people with authority, eg a policeman, doctor, vicar, teacher etc.

- **Service, Good news, Saviour, Authority**

# 113 JUMBLE SALE

**Equipment required**

Music, table, pile of objects – as many objects as there are players. Suitable objects are:

| | |
|---|---|
| Hats | Scarves |
| Books | Pencils |
| Cushions | Tennis balls |
| Shoes | Footballs |
| Boots | Racquets |
| Combs | Bats |
| Brushes | |

**To play**

The table of jumble should be on the opposite side of the room to the players. Play the music, then stop the tape unexpectedly. When this happens the entire group must dash for the table and grab an object. The first time this happens there will be something for everyone. Now play again, but remove one object. Whoever ends up without an object in the next round is out of the game – temporarily.

Continue to play until one player is left, triumphantly holding the one remaining object.

**Theme points – Sharing**

Ask the winner how he feels. Pretty good? Now ask the first person out how he felt about that. Not so good? Why? Talk about fairness and unfairness. They were grabbing a jumble of not-very-valuable objects. Ask them to imagine how it must feel to be a poor person or live in a poor country and see others 'getting there first' and 'grabbing the lot'. People in rich countries tend to feel more like the winner in the game – pretty good, most of the time. We should not forget the losers. Make a fuss here of your losers, they are just as important in this game as the winner! What does Jesus tell us about sharing, giving and riches? Go on from here. See also Acts 4:32–35.

• **Sharing, Giving, Poor, Riches**

# 114 USE YOUR LOAF!

**Equipment required**
Three slices off a cut loaf per four players. One plate for each group of four players.

**To play**
Announce that since everyone looks a bit peckish, you've decided to give them all a snack before you move on to the next part of your programme.

Have the group divide up into little clumps of four and sit them round so that their backs are to the other clumps and they can't see or hear what's going on between the others. If you have a surplus of one member make one foursome a fivesome and give that group an extra slice of bread. If you have a threesome left over, either join it yourself or give them two slices. Either way, every group should be handed a plate with one less slice of bread on it than there are group members. Now announce that they have three minutes to share the bread between them. (Don't give any more advice or information than this).

At the end of three minutes, call everyone together and ask volunteers from each group and tell you how they shared their bread.

**Theme points – Sharing**
Point out that nothing was said about equal shares. Did it occur to anyone to find out who was hungry and who wasn't, and apportion the bread according to need? We can become fixed in this concept of sharing meaning equal shares in order to be fair. Jesus meets our needs according to our needs, not our neighbours. John 6:11 can come in here, as everyone ate *their* fill. Jesus as the 'Bread of life' meets *our* needs whatever they are, large or small. Giving is linked here too: the world and its resources are unequally apportioned and we should be willing to give more of our over-large share to those in need.

- **Sharing, Giving, Bread of life, God knows Our needs**

# 115 LOADED!

**Equipment required**
Two tables and two identical sets of objects – about twelve per table.
Suggested items:

| | |
|---|---|
| Broom | Tennis racquet |
| Plastic bucket | Shoe |
| Football | Bag or tube of sweets |
| Hat | Cushion |
| Book | Magazine |
| Tennis ball | Balloon |

**To play**
Divide the group into two teams of no more than twelve per table (or
add a couple of objects so that there is a minimum of one object per
group member). The teams stand in line at the opposite end of the
room from the two tables.

At the word 'Go' one member of each team races to their table and
picks up any object at random. (It must be said that those who pick
the bucket first will have an advantage as it can be used to contain
other objects later on. Whether you point this out is up to you!) They
race back to their team and hand the objects to the next players. They
now run to the table and choose a second object, return to base and
pass on two objects: and so on until one team has cleared the table
and has everything at base. Dropped items must be picked up on the
spot. Make sure that the less able group members are near the front
of the team. They will have less to carry!

**Theme points – Sharing burdens**
See Galatians 6:2 and Matthew 5:41. The successful team was the one
in which the final member managed to get back to base with not only
his object, but everyone else's as well! Success in this game comes from
carrying one another's burden; sharing the load; working together.

● **Sharing burdens, Working together, Helping**

This is a silly game to be played for laughs. Don't spend to long on it.

**Equipment required**
Set of pieces of paper with one 'tricky task' written on each. Number them 1 to 5. Another set of solutions, similarly numbered. Paper and pencil for each group of players, piece of string.

*Tricky tasks*
1. Put a sheet of paper on the floor where no one can jump over it.
2. Put your left hand where your right hand can't reach it.
3. Pick up a piece of string and tie a knot in it without letting go of the ends.
4. Stay under water for five minutes.
5. Leave your pencil where everyone except you will be able to see it.

*Solutions*
1. Put the sheet of paper on the floor right up in the corner of the room.
2. Put your left hand on your right elbow and hold it.
3. Fold your arms and pick the string up, uncrossing your arms as you do so.
4. Get someone reliable to hold a cup of water in the air over your head for five minutes.
5. Balance your pencil on top of your head.

**To play**
Arrange the five tasks around the room. Divide your group into five small groups ideally with three to five members to a group, but pairs will work just as well. If you have less than ten players then pair them up and give them sixty seconds on each tricky task. Put the string near task three.

Each small group or pair of players is given a pencil and paper. Explain that round the room are five tricky tasks for them to tackle. One player in each group should write the numbers 1–5 down the side of the team paper. On the signal to start, each group will go to a different task and between them decide how to tackle it. One team member should write their solution against the appropriate number on the paper. Care should be taken not to let the other groups see or hear these ideas for solutions.

At the end of sixty seconds move the groups on to the next task on the list. After five minutes they should all have had a go at all of the challenges.

Now gather them all together and discuss their solutions. Did they manage to guess them all correctly? Show the prepared solutions.

**Theme points – Sharing burdens**
The 'tricky tasks' in this game were fun but silly. What happens when we get real problems to tackle (eg 'What exam options shall I take?', 'How can I play football or watch that video and still have time for youth group?') Was it easier to solve the problems by listening to other people's ideas? We should share our other problems too. We can share them with God in prayer. See 1 Peter 5:7.

Use this game also as an introduction to any Bible theme where someone is facing problems (eg King David, Joshua, Moses, Jonah etc). Go on to examine how they overcame their particular difficulties.

• **Sharing burdens, Working together, Prayer, Difficulties**

# 117 CHEAT!

**Equipment required**
None

**To play**
All the players sit round on the floor (not necessarily in a circle – a random pattern is best) with an arm span gap between them.

One player is 'It'. 'It' tags any seated player at random, and runs away. That player must get up and try to tag 'It' who dodges in and around the seated players. The chaser *must* follow 'It's' movements exactly; if he deviates the rest must shout, 'Cheat!' and the chaser must sit down.

'It' then tags another player. If 'It' is caught, the chaser takes over as 'It'. Keep it moving!

**Theme points – Sin**
The only way to win is to follow 'It' *exactly*. 'Cheating' is 'sin'! Sin is doing things our way not God's way. Sin breaks the rules.

• **Sin, Following, Cheating**

**Equipment required**
Three darts and dartboard; three ping-pong balls and jam jar; three tennis balls and bucket. Unless you have adequate supervision and extremely sensible players, the Velcro type of darts/board is probably safest!

**To play**
Everyone takes a turn at all three target games. You could have three teams and have the three games going in rotation until everyone has had a go at all three. With darts the aim is to score three bullseyes with three darts from a set distance. Make sure it is far enough away to be difficult! With ping-pong balls the aim is to bounce three balls off the table and into the jar. With tennis balls the aim is to bounce three balls from a set distance into the bucket. Players get one point for each bullseye.

**Theme points – Sinners**
The teams' *potential* score was nine times the number of team members. (Work this out!) Did any team score the maximum? Probably not! Tell them that therefore they are all sinners and have sinned $x$ times today already! ($x$ is the potential maximum score less the team's actual score.) Explain that the words 'sin' and 'sinner' came from the Old English 'synner' which is an archery term for someone who misses the mark. 'All have sinned and fall short of the glory of God' (Roman 3:23, NIV). But although we don't always reach the standards that we – or God – would want in our lives we can always go back and try again. Our God is loving and forgiving. See 1 John 1:8–10: 'He will forgive us our sins and purify us from all our wrongdoing.'

You may prefer to play just one of the games to make the same point.

- **Sinners, Forgiveness**

# 119 WHAT'S THE TIME, SOLOMON?

**Equipment required**
None

**To play**
One player is chosen to start the game as Solomon. He or she stands on one side of the room facing the rest of the children. On the far side of the room is a row of chairs, one less than the total number of players.

The children chant, 'What's the time, Solomon?' and Solomon announces that it is, for example, hopping, clapping, shouting, dancing, jumping or singing time. Any noisy or vigorous activity will do.

The players must all obey until Solomon raises a royal hand to make them stop. They then chant again, 'What's the time, Solomon?'

Play continues like this until Solomon, choosing his moment carefully, slips in the response, 'Quiet time!' whereupon *all* the players, including Solomon, must rush to a chair and sit down – quietly. Whoever does not have a chair plays Solomon for the next round.

**Theme points – Solomon**
God spoke to Solomon at night while he was asleep – a quiet time. We need to sit and be still and quiet as well if we want to hear God speak.

- **Solomon, Listening, Hearing, Quiet Time**

# 120 BOAT RACING

**Equipment required**
Plastic beaker of water for each player, two towels.

**To play**
Divide the group into two teams. The teams sit in a line facing each other. The team leader is given a towel. All team members are given a beaker of water to hold.

On the word 'Go' the leaders put the towel round their necks, drink the water in their beaker and up-end the empty beaker on their heads. Keeping the beaker balanced there they pass the towel to the next player.

Play passes down the line in this fashion until all the players have an empty beaker balanced on their heads. The winning team is the first one with all beakers empty and balanced. No hands!

**Theme points – Thirst**
Point out that the children had to drink the cup of water to enable their team to win. It's easier when we're thirsty.

Jesus said, 'Whoever is thirsty should come to me and drink' (John 7:37). What did he mean? He also told us, of ordinary water, 'Whoever drinks this water will be thirsty again, but whoever drinks the water that I will give him will never be thirsty again' (John 4:13).

• **Thirst, Living water, Holy Spirit**

# 121 CRACKERS!

**Equipment required**
One cream cracker per person, jug of water, plastic beakers.

**To play**
Divide the group into two teams, sitting in a line facing each other.
The team leader is given a packet (or half a packet) of cream crackers.

On the word 'Go' the team leaders take one cracker each, eat them,
and then whistle to prove their mouths really are empty. (You will
need two referees for this.) Upon producing an audible 'whistle' the
packet is passed to the next player in line, who must do the same.

The first team to complete the task must all jump up and whistle
together to win. Suggest a chorus for a tune.

**Theme points – Thirst**
Ask, 'Who is thirsty?' Produce the jug and beakers for everyone. Talk
about what it is like being thirsty, what sort of situations produce thirst
and what sort of thirst Jesus meant. How do we quench our thirst?
Jesus said, 'Whoever is thirsty should come to me and drink' (John
7:37) What did he mean? He also told us, of ordinary water, 'Whoever
drinks this water will be thirsty again, but whoever drinks the water
that I will give him will never be thirsty again' (John 4:13).

- **Thirst, Living water, Holy Spirit**

133

# 122 CONVEYOR BELT

**Equipment required**
Two deep bags or sacks to hold about eight or nine objects such as:

A watch
A tin of baked beans
A personal stereo
A pair of binoculars
A toothbrush
A camera

Aim at a good mix of valuable and not so valuable objects. One of the objects should be a clay flower pot half-filled with coins. Make sure the coins are not visible or put a crumpled piece of newspaper in the top.

**To play**
The children sit facing a table. You sit behind the table with the bag of objects on one side and the empty bag on the other side. Objects must only be visible in transit from one bag to the other bag.

Tell the group that they are going to see a procession of objects over a 'conveyor belt'. They must concentrate and remember all that they see. Try a bit of 'patter' about each object if you like (eg 'Now here's something to make you smile' for the camera).

When you finish say that you now want them to remember all the objects and list them in order of value with the most valuable first and the least valuable last. The children can either do this collectively and you write up a list visible to all, or they can make their own lists and you can compile a 'master list' from these when they finish.

**Theme points – Treasure within**
Arrange the objects on the table with those objects commonly agreed to be most valuable at one end and the least valuable at the other. The flower pot *should* end up near the bottom of the scale. Now tip out the contents! Point out that they were judging by outward appearances to arrive at their valuations. God doesn't do this – he sees what's **inside** and judges by that. 2 Corinthians 4:7 speaks of this treasure within: 'We who have this spiritual treasure are like common clay pots.'

- **Appearances, Judgment, Treasure within**

# 123 THREESOMES

**Equipment required**

Groups of three chairs dotted around the room. There should be one less group of three than the number of threesomes playing. If space is short then one chair per threesome will do. You will need a number of players that is divisible by three. Co-opt helpers and leaders if necessary. If you really cannot avoid someone being surplus then give him a role to play – blowing the starting whistle for example – and he can swap with a player next time round. The game is played in elimination rounds.

You will also need a set of slips of paper (one per player) with 'threesome' words written on them (eg water – ice – steam). Ideas for sets:

Water – ice – steam
Bread – toast – sandwich
Leaf – branch – tree
Knife – fork – spoon
Feather – wing – bird
Sun – moon – stars

**To play**

Jumble up the words and drop a few in each of the four corners of the room. On the word 'Go' all the players must run and grab one slip of paper. They must now try to find their two partners. When a threesome has been formed they must then rush and sit on a group of three chairs (or all sit on one chair on each other's knees if you are short of space). The threesome left standing is eliminated and you play again – removing one set of chairs and one set of slips. You could substitute a different set of slips if you can think of enough permutations!

**Theme points – Trinity**

Ask what was the basic principle of the game. The answer is 'threes': three closely related words, three players, three chairs. Ask if anyone can think of a Bible-based threesome that you could have used – but didn't. Father – Son – Holy Spirit (the **Trinity** should be mentioned).

Think about your other threesomes; some were more closely related than others. Water, ice and steam are same substance in three different forms. Launch your Trinity study from this point. Father, Son and Holy Spirit and three persons but one God.

- **Trinity, One God**

# 124 TRINITY LINK-UP TAG

**Equipment required**
None

**To play**
Play a game of 'Link-up tag' (see game 36) but with the players linked in threes instead of twos.

**Theme points – Trinity**
Trinity means Tri-unity – three working together as one. This is what the children had to try and do and is what the 'Trinity' is about – Father/Son/Spirit together as one God.

   Play other 'threesome' games and have the children look for the common theme.

- **Trinity, One God**

# 125 TRIPLE TARGETS

**Equipment required**
Buckets, coins, ping-pong balls, jam jars, pack of cards.

**To play**
Have three teams doing the three tasks. No team moves on until the tasks have been completed!

*Task 1*
Drop three 2p coins into a bucket of water containing three 1p coins so that the 2p coins cover the 1p coins. Every time a coin lands in the right place leave it there and retrieve the misplaced one(s). Team members take it in turns to drop coins until all the 1ps are covered.

*Task 2*
Bounce three ping-pong balls off a table-top and into a jam jar.

*Task 3*
Stand with one foot each side of a bucket and hold a playing card against the bridge of your nose (long side against your nose). Let it go. Take it in turns and get three into the bucket.

**Theme points – Trinity**
Play this in conjunction with game 41. Ask what the games had in common (it's 'threes'). Then go on to talk about the Trinity.

   Persistence and patience were needed to complete the tasks. How do we overcome difficulties in life? As well as persistence and prayer we need help from each other and from God. Pick up the theme of prayer.

- **Trinity, One God, Difficulties, Prayer**

# 126 TRIPLETS

**Equipment required**
A list of categories such as:

| | |
|---|---|
| Planets | Composers |
| Flowers | Artists |
| Wild animals | Countries |
| Colours | Girls' names |
| Prime ministers | Boys' names |
| Trees | Fish |
| Food | Capital cities |

**To play**
Divide the group into two teams. Alternating between the teams, ask each team member in turn to name three things in one of your categories. You may wish to narrow the categories down, eg:

Three yellow flowers
Three girls' names beginning with 'D'
Three evergreen trees

You can normally pitch the questions to suit the ability of the individual so that it is a fair contest for everyone.

As soon as you have given the child their category the opposing team chant slowly, 'One! Two! Three!' Time is up on the count of three.

See which team manages to come up with the most threesomes.

**Theme points – Trinity**
Ask who can tell you who is the most famous threesome of all. Someone may suggest the **Trinity!**

Alternatively play this game with other 'threesome' games and ask the group for the common link.

● **Trinity, One God**

This is another version of 'Sticky Toffee'.

**Equipment required**
None

**To play**
One player is chosen as 'It'; the rest are frogs. For a quicker game have two players as 'It', especially if your group is larger than ten or twelve.

Any player who is tagged must crouch down, frog fashion, and go, 'Ribbit! Ribbit!' loudly to show that he is 'stuck in the bog'. A free frog may release stuck frogs by leap-frogging over them. The game ends when the bog is full and all the frogs are 'Ribbiting' with no one left to release them. The last frog left hopping free may become 'It' for the next round.

**Theme points – Trouble**
What sort of things bog us down in our Christian lives? How can we call out for help when we are in trouble? Who can we call on? We should be able to ask our friends for help – both practical and in prayer. We should also be able to ask Jesus for help – he's promised to hear us when we pray or are in trouble. He sets captives free! See also Psalm 45:1.

● **Trouble, Captivity/Sin, Help, Prayer, Release/captives**

**Equipment required**

A list of ten words, each with three definitions, only one of which is true. The words need to be written large enough to be read by the whole group: the definitions should be on three separate small slips of paper. Take care not to jumble them up and keep your master list to hand! It's fun to make up your own word lists, but here are some examples:

1. Wow-wow

   a. The doggie in the window
   b. A gibbon from Sumatra
   c. A girl in a pink cat-suit

2. Saraband

   a. A headband worn by pirates
   b. A pop group led by a girl called Sara
   c. A stately Spanish dance

3. Timoneer

   a. A wart on the ear lobe
   b. Ship's lookout or helmsman
   c. Irish boy who lives up the road

4. Yaffle

   a. To waffle on, speaking nonsense
   b. A green woodpecker
   c. An item of riding tackle

5. Skulpin

   a. A remedy for head injuries
   b. A type of hat pin
   c. piky fish with large heads

6. Heriot

   a. A small boy's chariot
   b. A fine or tax
   c. A Yorkshire vet

7. Conventicle

   a. A secret gathering
   b. A gathering of small nuns
   c. A small nun's gathering

8. Salmagundie

a. A little known Eastern author
b. A mixture of meat and chopped-up eggs
c. A Scots expression for 'Sally – pass my underwear'

9. Whigmaleerie

a. An Irish banshee
b. Trinket or gewgaw
c. Lively gig danced by bald Scotsmen in hair pieces

10. Eglantine

a. A sweet pudding made with eggs and gelatine
b. A sweet briar rose
c. A girl's name, like 'Clementine'

The true definitions are 1b, 2c, 3b, 4b, 5c, 6b, 7a, 8b, 9b, 10b.

**To play**

Divide the group into two teams sitting facing each other. In turn give the teams a 'set' of a word plus three definitions.

Team A begins with one member holding up the word for all to see. Three others read out the definitions as convincingly as possible – encourage them to ham this up.

Team B has to decide which is the true definition. If they are right you award them a point. If they are wrong, Team A can then choose a definition and try to gain a point.

Play then passes to Team B with another word and set of definitions. Continue to play until all the words have been used. Make sure all the group members have a chance at holding up a word or reading a definition. If the teams are large they can work in pairs.

**Theme points – Truth**

Ask how they knew which were the true answers. Some definitions were obviously false, but others were confusing. Ultimately they had to rely on your word for it – you had the list of true answers.

If we want to know the truth – about life, death, Jesus, the way to God etc – we have to rely on the Word of God. We can rely on the Bible for true answers. We also have to beware of false prophets – people who tell us things that sound OK but in fact are not Bible truths. We need to know for ourselves what the Bible says – just as you needed to look some words up in the dictionary to be sure of the answers.

• **Truth, Bible, False prophets**

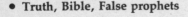

# 129 'FEELY' RACE

**Equipment required**
Pillow-case, tied firmly at the top, containing twenty small objects (see 'Funny feelings', game 9, for suggestions). Pens and paper.

**To play**
Place the pillow-case on a chair or table at the far side of the room. Divide the group into teams of up to ten players. Give each team a pen and paper and line them up on the opposite side of the room to the pillow-case.

On the signal to begin, the teams simultaneously send one team member to feel the pillow-case and identify an object.

As soon as an object is identified, the team members run back and the team write down that object on the paper. Another team member now runs to identify another object and so on.

Either play until one team has a list of all twenty objects or play for a set time limit. The winning team is the one with the most complete list. Tip out the pillow-case at the end.

**Theme points – Understanding**
Identifying objects by touch alone is not as easy as when we can use all our senses, including sight. It is not easy to understand everything about Jesus or God because we can't see him – we can only 'touch' him through the Bible, the Holy Spirit and other Christians. One day we will see and understand completely – as the players were able to identify everything when they saw the objects 'face to face'. See 1 Corinthians 13:12.

Pick up the themes of blindness/sight, disabilities, discernment. Discernment is 'telling things apart'. How do we tell good from bad; the way of Jesus from the way of evil?

● **Understanding, Blindness/sight, Disability, Discernment**

**Equipment required**
Balloon and rolled-up newspaper 'hockey sticks' or drinking straws and a ping-pong ball. Four chairs.

**To play**
You need two teams plus one or two volunteer 'reporters' who will leave the room temporarily or be blindfolded and sit on a chair facing the wall.

The two teams play a game of 'Balloon hockey' or any similar noisy, competitive game. A good variation is ping-pong blow football. Use drinking straws and have four chairs placed in pairs for goals.

The players each have a straw and crawl about on hands and knees blowing a ping-pong ball and trying to score goals.

The reporters are shut outside the room or are blindfolded and sat on a chair facing the wall. They must listen to the game.

Play three minutes or so each way. Now ask your reporters to describe the game giving as much detail as possible – write it down if you like. Don't let the players interrupt yet!

Now ask the players if the reporters got it right! Did they get the names of the goal scorers? Did they get the score right? Did they get the details of the finer points of play – the near-misses etc? Why not?

**Theme points – Witnesses**
Paul talks about eye-witnesses to the Resurrection. They were there, they saw Jesus and they got it right, so the Bible is not just hearsay! You could talk about the difference it makes having a reliable 'first-hand' account of a game and of the resurrection of Jesus. It means that we can talk about it authoritatively ourselves. We can be 'witnesses' as well.

- **Witnesses, Resurrection/eye-witnesses**

# 131 READY RACE

**Equipment required**

Large quantity of dressing-up clothes. If possible, duplicate similar items, eg two men's suit jackets, two nylon nighties etc. Possible clothes include:

Men's jackets
Nylon nighties
All kinds of hats
Woolly cardigans
Mittens
Scarves
Wellington boots
Sunglasses
Baby bonnets
Shirts
Dressing gowns

Frilly blouses
Aprons
Rubber gloves
Ties
Shorts
T-shirts
Sandals
Slippers
Bed socks
Swimsuits

You will also need a list of occupations, eg:

Spring cleaning
Farming
Getting married/being a bridesmaid
Olympic running
Building a snowman
Sun-bathing
Entering a 'bonny baby' show
Going to school

Adjust your bagful of clothes so that it is possible to find at least six garments – three per team – suitable for each occupation.

**To play**

Divide your group into two teams. Ask if they've ever heard anyone say they 'haven't a thing to wear!' They are now going to find out what it feels like! In the centre of the room, tip out your pile of clothes, boots, shoes etc. Explain that each team must send two players at a time, in pairs; the four will be given sixty seconds to plunder the pile and dress one of each pair as appropriately as possible for the occupation they are given. At the end of that time the dressed-up players must act out their occupations and the rest of the group must guess what they are 'ready' to do. The best-dressed player scores five team points, the other scores three.

When all the team members have had a turn, add up the total score and see which team wins. Scoring can be decided by popular acclaim. If both candidates are equally well-dressed give them both five points.

## Theme points – Worry

The game is all about a frantic scramble to try and find something to wear. Jesus tells us not to worry about things like this – to trust God to provide for us. See Matthew 6:24–34.

Being dressed appropriately means you're ready to go – whether to a wedding, a party, school, or whatever. What is it we are told to be prepared for? Jesus is coming again and we don't know when. We are warned to be ready 'clothed in righteousness'. What does this mean?

- **Worry, Readiness, Clothed in righteousness, Trusting**

# MULTI-PURPOSE GAMES

These games are designed to be flexible in terms of theme. You can tailor them to fit your needs according to the points you are making. One or two themes are used to demonstrate how the games can be tailored to a teaching point; you are then left to substitute your own as required.

# 1 ACTING UP

**Equipment required**
None

**To play**
One player leaves the room and the others choose a word (an adjective) which can be acted, eg happily, carefully, angrily, etc. The player returns and has to guess what word the others have chosen. He does this by asking members of the group in turn – or, if you like, the whole group together – to perform an action in the manner of the word.

It may be helpful to display a list of actions eg:

a. Stand on a chair and wave to me.
b. Pick up a book and start reading.
c. Get up and hop round the room.
d. Shake hands with your neighbours.
e. Get up and walk round the room backwards.
f. Clap your hands five times.
g. Take your shoes off and put them on again.
h. Get up and turn round three times quickly.

The player can then just say, 'Susan – please do c.' As soon as he guesses the word, he rejoins the group. Someone else leaves the room and the players choose a new word to act.

**Theme points**
Let the children play this a few times to get the idea and then say that the next word will be related to your theme for the day. You then introduce your theme word. It could be 'blindly' – on the theme of spiritual blindness. Discuss how the group acted 'blindly' and how this relates to how we act when we suffer from spiritual blindness. The word could be 'angrily'. Discuss what effect anger has on our behaviour, and why the Bible tells us to let go of our anger. Forgiveness also comes in here.

You may have to think hard to think of an appropriate word to convey your theme, but it can usually be done! Opposites can work well, eg 'fearfully' links with the theme 'fear not'. How fear affects our actions (in the game) can lead into the Bible's message to 'fear not' and the freedom this brings.

● **Blindness/sight, Anger, Forgiveness, Fear**

# 2 BANANAS

**Equipment required**
None

**To play**
One player leaves the room and the other players choose a 'key' word. This can be an object (eg chair, motorbike, donkey) or an action (eg caring, laughing, crying etc).

The player returns and by asking questions to the group members in turn, tries to discover the key word. The group members must answer the question, incorporating the key word but substituting 'Bananas' in their answer. So if the key word is 'donkey' the dialogue might go like this.

Question: 'What's the weather like today?'
Answer: 'It's wet and cold, I wouldn't want to ride a banana today.'
Question: 'How did you get here this morning?'
Answer: 'I rode my bike, not my banana.'

**Theme points**
Let the group play this a couple of times then introduce your 'theme' words. These could be family and then church, or water followed by baptism.

If you tell the group that the last two words are going to relate to the theme of the day, you should end up with some useful questions and answers to provide a springboard for your study and discussion theme.

# 3 CORNERS

**Equipment required**

This game needs four teams of two to six or so players. Each team needs an identification colour. Coloured 'team bands' are ideal, but large sticky labels in four colours will work quite well. Or you could provide each child with a safety pin and a piece of paper about 15 cm square on which to write, with an appropriate felt pen, their team colour. They then can pin their labels on to their clothes.

Each team is assigned a corner of the room as 'home-base'. The corners should also be labelled red, blue, yellow etc.

You also need a long list of questions. Base these around your theme.

**To play**

The quiz-master stands in the middle of the room and puts a question to a member of, say, the red corner. If the child answers correctly he moves to the next corner. He keeps being asked more questions (and moves round the room) until he answers wrongly, in which case he remains in the corner at which he has now landed. The quiz-master then asks a member of the next team a question. If a player manages to answer four questions correctly and arrives back at home-base in one go, he sits on the floor and waits for the rest of the team to arrive. The first team to get all its members back to home-base is the winner.

**Theme points**

This game is a painless way of going over previous theme work. It can be played purely for fun by using questions from a 'Trivial pursuit' game. Follow up with theme questions for a second round.

# 4 DECISIONS

This is another very simple quiz game that can be used for revision. It can be useful to play two rounds, the first for fun (with silly and trick questions) and the second for introducing your theme or re-capping on previously studied material. It is a useful game to play as an introduction to a study of a too-familiar story.

## Equipment required

Two chairs placed in two corners of the room, Tape a piece of paper to the back of each one, one saying 'True', the other 'False'. A set of statements for each round of the game, eg:

1. Armadillos are anteaters T
2. Monkeys are nuts T
   (Monkey nuts!)
3. A kilo of lead is heavier than a kilo of feathers F
4. Whales are fishes F
5. The Queen has four grand-children F
6. Koalas are marsupials T

Or:

1. Jesus was born in Nazareth F
2. Herod was the Prime Minister F
3. Three wise men visited the baby F
   (The Bible doesn't tell us how many there were!)
4. The wise men brought gold, frankincense and myrrh T
5. A star over the stable showed where Jesus was T
6. Shepherds visited the baby as well T

Whatever statements you have on your list make sure you indicate 'T' and 'F' for your own benefit – it's easy to get confused yourself in the heat of the moment.

## To play

Line the group up in two teams. A member of each team steps forward; you read your first statement. The two team members race to sit on whichever chair they consider appropriate – True or False – to respond to your statement. A point is scored for each correct answer and the first team member to sit on the correct chair gets a bonus point.

## Theme points

When you come to round two announce you're going to find out just how much they know about – (whatever is your chosen topic). Get all the children to tell you whether they think the statement is true or false. If it's false get the team to tell you what they think the true statement should have been.

Word your statements carefully, cover your topic comprehensively, and your group will learn an awful lot without really trying!

# 5 DUMB SHOW

**Equipment required**
List of words on slips of paper.

**To play**
This game is played as a mime relay race. It is useful to have a strong-minded and eagle-eyed referee (with a copy of the word list) for each team to prevent cheating in the form of speaking or mouthing words.

The teams sit in semi-circles in front of their referee. On the word 'Go' one member of each team jumps up and is shown a word on the list. Take care to show only one word (or you can whisper the word). He then has to mime that word to the team, who have to try and guess what the word is. When they have identified the word another team member jumps up and is told the next word. Play progresses until one team has identified the complete list. Sit the teams on opposite sides of the room so that they cannot see or hear the others in action. It is in their own interests not to shout the answers too loudly!

**Theme points**
This depends entirely on how you choose to compose your word list. For a simple revision quiz you might base your list on the previous session's study. For a study of Jonah use the word list: whale, storm, overboard, repent, sack-cloth . . . etc. Almost any Bible-based story, parable or incident can be used as a theme base in this way.

• **Jonah**

# 6 GIVE US A CLUE

This is a mime game which is probably familiar to most children. It is a good way of introducing a memory verse or short theme text, eg 'Ask and you will receive, seek and you will find, knock and the door will be opened to you' (Matthew 7:7).

**To play**

This game can be played with the whole group together and one person miming the text, or you can play with two teams, the teams taking it in turns to try to guess their text within a time limit of, say, two or three minutes.

One player is given a slip of paper with the text written on it. He then attempts to convey the message to his team.

There are a few accepted 'code' signals which may be used. These are:

*Number of words:* One finger held up in air for each word
*Number of syllables* in any given word: Hold the appropriate number of fingers on one hand to the elbow of the other arm.
*Short words/long words:* Hold hands close together or far apart.
*'Sounds like':* Hold ear, then mime.

**Theme points**

This game can be used simply to engrave a memory verse on the minds of all those present or to present a theme. To do this select several texts which have a similar theme, eg Matthew 5:14, Matthew 5:16, John 9:5 and John 1:5 all refer to 'light'. If your Bible study only gives you one useful text for this game, try using a concordance to look up the key theme word and find some more.

When you get really good at this you can even tell chapter and verse in mime as well. Thumbs over shoulder means 'past' ie Old Testament: pointing forwards means 'New Testament'. Then a number of fingers can indicate the first, second, third or thirty-ninth (!) book. (Bibles allowed for reference at your discretion!)

By the time the groups have deciphered your texts, they will all be well into the topic; ask them what the common theme seems to be – and take your study on from there.

You could also use popular hymn and chorus titles with common theme links.

# 7 INSTANT ART

**Equipment required**
Paper, pens for drawing, list of things to draw. Base these on your theme, eg
  For Noah write:

| | |
|---|---|
| Boat | Rain |
| Two elephants | Wind |
| Two eagles | Mountains |
| Two lions | Dove |

For Jonah write:

| | |
|---|---|
| Ship | Worm |
| Storm | Wind |
| Large fish | Sun |
| Vine | |

You could begin with a list of words unrelated to the theme, to give the children an idea of how to play, then announce that the final six or eight words will be related to your theme study. (This can either be an introduction to the theme or a game-break in the middle of a session.)

**To play**
Divide the group into teams. Each team has a table equipped with pencil and paper. At the signal to start one member from each team runs to the leader who shows them the first word on the list. They then run back to their teams and draw the word. When someone guesses what it is, another team member runs to be shown the next word. Take care that only one word can be seen (have them on separate pieces of paper for example) and make sure that both teams have all the words eventually. The team members should be careful not to shout their answers too loudly or they will give away clues to the other team. The first team to guess the lot is the winner.

**Theme points**
This is a very simple way of introducing a storyline – you can ask who can guess what the theme or story is to be. Or it can be used to re-cap on the sequence of events in a story.

# 8 LIGHTNING LISTS

**Equipment required**

A watch with a second hand. List of 'trigger' words eg:

Colours                     Fish species
Planets                     British birds
Yellow flowers              Countries of the world
Marsupials                  Languages
British Prime Ministers

A score-board of some kind.

**To play**

You can play this either in teams, alternating between the teams with trigger words, or simply go round the whole group in turn.

Appoint a time-keeper and explain that you will be giving a key word and the team member whose turn it is will then have sixty seconds to name as many things/associated words as possible. Get the groups to count aloud as the player lists his words.

**Theme points**

The theme depends on your key words. You may like to play this once for fun, with a word list similar to that above, and then follow up with a word list associated with your theme. This could be on Bible topics (eg commandments, parables, books of the Bible, people in the Bible, beatitudes, places in the Bible, prophets, miracles of Jesus) or you may have a theme such as 'responsibility' or 'praise'. In that case announce that your last key word is, for example, 'praise' and get the whole group to list as many associated words as possible in sixty seconds. Write these up and you will have a flying start to your session. Make sure that your master list of trigger words contains both very easy categories (eg breeds of dog) as well as the more esoteric ones (like Prime Ministers) and be sensitive in allocating them so that differences in age and ability are levelled out.

- **Bible, Praise**

# 9 MEMORY VERSE SIT

**Equipment required**

Roll of wallpaper or lining paper cut into long strips 20 cm deep. Write your memory verse out on a strip of paper and mark it into as many words or phrases as you have players. You can play with one set of words and one team of players. Alternatively play as a team competition with two (or more) sets of words. Write one version in red and one in blue if you are playing the team version.

**To play**

Unroll one strip and have two players hold the ends so that the words can be seen and read. Give the children thirty seconds to repeat and memorise the verse, then cut the strip(s) up into the requisite number of pieces.

Put one chair – or two for the team version – at the front of the room. The jumbled words are put at the far side of the room. (For the team version use two sets of words, jumbled together.)

On the signal to start, everyone must rush and grab a word at random. (For the team version they then sort themselves out into a red and a blue team.) Everyone must now sort themselves out into a reassembled memory verse. They then sit on the chair and on each others' knees in correct sequence and hold their words up over their heads. As soon as the last player is seated the whole team must shout the words in turn to produce a complete memory verse.

If you play the one team version, you may like to time them and give them the opportunity to play again and 'beat the clock' later on.

# 10 QUIZ ROUNDERS

**Equipment required**

Chairs for bases – three for teams of four or five members, four for six or seven members and so on. Arrange the chairs in a large circle. You will also need two lists of quiz questions – one of silly and trivia-type questions, the other based on your Bible theme. Have enough questions for all players to have at least two goes at 'batting' for their team.

Alternatively, compile a list of true and false statements relating to your theme text. For example

1. Jesus was born in Nazareth F
2. Jesus was born in Bethlehem T

Make a 'bat' from a piece of card with a red T on one side and green F on the other.

**To play**

Divide the group into two teams and explain that they are going to be playing rounders with a difference. You will be the 'bowler' and you will be lobbing some fast questions instead of fast balls! The teams take it in turns to 'bat'.

Begin with your trivia quiz to give everyone the idea of how to play; keep the questions easy.

The first player from Team A answers the first question. If he is right – he goes to the first chair and sits on it; if he is wrong, he goes to the back of the team to try again later. The next player – from Team B – has a turn. If correct, he moves to the first chair and the player from Team A moves up to the second chair – and so on. The teams score a point for each player who completes the chair circuit.

Keep it moving fast and pitch the questions to the ability of the individual.

When the first round of questions has been completed announce that for the final batting you will be asking questions based on your Bible theme – so the winners will be the ones who stayed awake recently! Then go into your final round.

If you play the 'true or false?' version, the bowler reads out a statement from the list and the batsman must swiftly hold up and display whichever side of the 'bat' (T or F) he considers appropriate. Play continues as in the previous method.

**Theme points**

This is an adaptable quiz game because it can be played with small or large numbers. It also means that children who do not normally excel at rounders get a chance to do so in a different way – particularly if you are careful to give everyone at least one question they can get right.

# 11 RUSH HOUR

**Equipment required**

List of true and false Bible statements for your theme point. For the story of Moses (Exodus 1–3) one might have:

1. Moses grew up in Egypt T
2. Moses was adopted by a princess T
3. Moses married Zipporah T
4. Moses was King of Egypt F
5. Moses saw a burning bush T
6. The Lord spoke to Moses from the bush T
7. The Lord told Moses to rescue the Hebrews T
8. Moses agreed straightaway to do what God said F
9. Moses asked God what to say to the king T
10. God said, 'I am who I am' T

Begin with a silly round or two of the game to give the group the idea of how to play. Then play a round which incorporates your 'theme' statements following the pattern of the example above.

**To play**

The whole group stands on one side of the room touching the wall. A caller is chosen – or a leader can call – and is given a subject, eg 'birds'. The caller stands in the middle of the playing space and calls, for example,

'Birds fly'
'Birds lay eggs'
'Eagles are birds'
'Birds have feathers'
'Robins fly'

If the statement is true the players must rush to the far side of the room and touch that wall. If, however, the caller slips in a false statement (eg 'Carrots fly') anyone who moves a muscle or starts running across the room is out.

Keep the calling as fast as possible. When the group gets going a surprising number will stop thinking and just dash first and think later.

Begin with a silly round or two to give the group the idea of how to play. Then play your theme version as a finale, with everyone participating.

**Theme points**

This can be a simple theme revision or introduction game. It can also raise points of thinking about 'following the crowd' and the importance of thinking for ourselves before we act, not just copying everyone else. Theme of truth/falsehood and how we distinguish the one from the other can also be brought out.

# 12 TIC-TAC-TOE-TALS

This is a version of noughts and crosses, played with people and chairs, and provides a popular alternative to a straightforward revision quiz. It can be used with any theme or subject base – you provide the questions, based around any theme or topic you like.

## Equipment required

Nine chairs arranged in three lines of three, all facing forwards.

Two sets of half a dozen A4 sheets of paper or card with a large 0 or X written on them, one lot in red the other in blue. The teams can make their own, or you can prepare them in advance. List of questions. You may wish to have some 'silly' questions (based, for example on the statements given in 'Decisions' – multi-purpose game 4) as well as questions relating to your theme.

## To play

Divide your group into two teams of five or more. Boys versus girls can be popular, but use your discretion – younger children enjoy this but older ones can prefer to be mixed.

The teams are asked questions in turn from your master list. Play the 'silly' round first. If they get the answer right, the player who answered correctly takes a card and sits on a chair of his choice. If he gets the answer wrong, the other team may answer the question and hope to gain an extra seat. The players who are seated on the grid may not answer further questions! It's up to the rest of the team now – and they must also choose where to seat each winning member. The first team to complete a line of 0s or Xs is the winner.

This game moves fast and works best played several times over with the winning team being 'best of three' rounds. If you pitch your questions to the age and abilities of the remaining contestants, everyone has a fair chance of getting a seat at some point.

## Theme points

This game can be linked with any theme you like.

# 13 UNSCRAMBLE

### Equipment required
Two sets of cards or pieces of paper with one letter written on each card, which can be rearranged to spell out your theme word.

For each team participating in an indoor version you need:

a. A chair with needle and thread – needle to be threaded.
b. A table with six building blocks to be stacked – and stay stacked!
c. Another chair or table with a jug of water and cup – cup to be filled and water drunk.
d. Another table – to be crawled under.
e. A pile of jumbled theme word letters, face down, on a chair – one to be taken at random and rushed back to team.

For each team participating in an outdoor version you need:

a. A hoop – to be passed right over body.
b. Bean bag/cushion – to balance on head and run to next obstacle. (No hands!)
c. Skipping rope – must be skipped over five times.
d. Pile of potatoes, tablespoon – one potato to be picked up, using spoon only, and run to next obstacle point.
e. Bucket of water, cups – two cups to be filled, one in each hand, and run to final obstacle point and pour contents into jug or bucket.
f. A pile of jumbled theme word letters, face down, on a chair or table – one to be taken at random and rushed back to team.

### To play
This is a straightforward obstacle relay race. The teams line up at home base and in turn run to complete the obstacle course and grab a letter to form the word. Play continues and the teams collect letters until one team can identify the word. If a team thinks it knows the word, they all sit down and shout it out in unison. If they still have not collected all the letters, and if they are correct, then both teams may now dash for the remaining letters and see which team can be the first to set the letters out in correct order at home base.

### Theme points
This is straightforward; tell them that they have unscrambled the point behind the day's session, to keep it in mind as you go on into your study/thinking time.

# 14 WHO AM I?

**Equipment required**
None

**To play**
One player must leave the room; the rest of the group decide who he is going to be on his return.

The player comes back in and asks the group members in turn questions about his identity, eg 'Am I a musician?' 'Am I a woman?' etc. He has twenty questions and they may only be answered with a 'Yes' or 'No'.

**Theme points**
If you are about to do a Bible study which focuses on a particular person in the Bible, allow them to play the game for fun for a few rounds and then when you are ready to end the game tell the group that the next character will be the one you will be discussing after the game.

Alternatively you could run the game along the theme point lines suggested for game 15 – 'Whose hat?' – and all the characters acted out will have a theme in common. For example – life-guard, bank manager and stamp collector have the common theme – saving. This leads into another kind of saving – salvation.

- **Bible, Saving, Salvation**

# 15 WHOSE HAT?

**Equipment required**

Bagful of assorted hats – enough for every player minus one. Try to have as wide a variety and as many 'silly' hats as possible. Tape recorder and music tape. List of occupations that fit your theme – write these on individual slips of paper. For the theme of caring you might list nurse, doctor, vet, teacher, dentist, shepherd. For 'security' you might list policeman, life-guard, lollipop person, firefighter, soldier, traffic warden.

**To play**

Ask the group if they have ever heard the expression, 'Which hat are you wearing today?' This means, 'What role are you playing?' A boy can, for example, be a son, a brother, a schoolboy, a boy scout or a prefect, depending on what 'hat' he wears. Tip out the bagful of hats and announce that you have got a few hats for the children to try for size. Everyone should sit in a circle with each player facing the back of the player in front. They need to sit fairly close to each other and one player will begin the game hatless. When the music starts each player must grab the hat from the head of the person in front and put it on his own head. This chain of hat-passing continues until the music stops.

You now announce that since one person is hatless you will have to give him a role to play. The hatless player is handed a slip of paper and must mime the occupation written on the piece of paper. When the rest of the group have guessed correctly, the music starts and the hats are passed again.

**Theme points**

Ask the group to identify what the occupations had in common, this will give the clue to your theme point.

• **Caring, Security**

# 16 WORDSEARCH RACE

### Equipment required

This game needs a fair amount of preparation but can be very useful as a revision quiz or to introduce a theme or Bible study. You will need to make up a wordsearch square of your own devising, containing all your key words. This is not as hard as it sounds! Use a large sheet of paper. Make a list of all the words (up to eight if you don't want it to be too hard) you want to incorporate and tick them off as you go. For John 15:1–10 you might list fire, Father, gardener, prune, vine, branches, fruit, remain. It is helpful to place the longer words first.

Fill the empty squares with random letters (you can just use X and Y to make it easy) and make a copy for each team playing. Write the words on separate pieces of paper, one complete set for each team. You need marker pens.

### To play

Pin each team's wordsearch up well away from the other's and divide the group into teams.

On the word 'Go' pairs of players from each team are given a word. They run to their puzzle and try to find their word on the grid. They ring it round with a marker pen, pin the word up next to the puzzle, and run back to the group. Then the next pair are given a word. Play continues until one team finds all the words. Pairing the players helps overcome literacy difficulties which might arise.

### Theme points

When using this game as a revision aid, ask who can remember where the words came from and ask the groups to tell you the full text as accurately as possible from memory. (You may then re-read the original version!) As an introductory game you can then say that you are now going to find out where the words come from and how they fit together, properly, in context.